Student Handbook

The Struggle for Civil Rights

(SNCC members being briefed before heading to Belzoni, MS; 1963 © Matt Herron/Take Stock / The Image Works)
Cover photo:
(Freedom School, Mississippi Summer Project 1964, © 1976 Matt Herron/Take Stock / The Image Works)

Dr. Jim Highland, John Carroll University
Dr. Harold McDougall, Howard University School of Law

July 2015
SG Publishing

Table of Contents

Introduction — 5
Ch. 1 Nonviolent Tension and Resistance — 29
Ch. 2 Philosophical Positions of the Factions — 33
Ch. 3 Introduction to Module I: *Dorchester 1963,*
The Struggle for Nonviolent Tension — 41
Ch. 4 Introduction to Module II: *Memphis 1966,*
The Struggle for Black Power — 47

Appendix I:
Civil Rights History
and the Long Road Already Traveled — 53

Appendix II:
Events, Institutions and Movements
Shaping Post-Brown v. Board of Education — 81

Appendix III:
Introduction to Highlander Folk School — 121

Appendix IV:
Primary Readings for
The Struggle For Civil Rights — 149

Introduction
The Struggle for Civil Rights

The Struggle for Civil Rights is a college-level, academic game set in 1963 and 1966 at key moments in the Civil Rights Movement. These moments are not the protests and boycotts which have made headlines, but the meetings and debates which were held as those protest activities were planned. They are the settings for debates and deliberations within the community of the Civil Rights Movement, regarding where and how to conduct protests. They are based on goals that are, generally speaking, similar, but supported by different ideas about what means should be employed to achieve those goals. The participants in these scenarios will agree with the need to end the Jim Crow laws of segregation, as well as the prejudices which support and extend the effects of those laws. But they will disagree about the means used to achieve those ends. This does not mean that one faction will advocate for their favorite means and against any others. They all realize the need for multiple approaches. But which approach is the best approach given the realities of the cultural and political landscape in 1963 and 1966? That is where they will differ. To be sure, they will also disagree on some longer-term goals and their visions for the future activities of the Movement, but the meetings in 1963 and 1966 will focus on debating the relative merit of various proposed activities, given the realities of the struggle for civil rights in 1963 and 1966.

As such, the academic game, while set at key historical moments, is not just a simulation of those moments. Yes, the conditions and characters resemble those of the historical moment, but the game requires you to study, understand and put into practice the philosophical foundations for the different methods of bringing about change which were debated at these times. You will need to read the **Philosophical Positions of the Factions** to better understand these positions for your own character and for how you will interact with others. Briefly stated, all of the methods are nonviolent. One (NAACP) takes a more legal approach, advocating for legislation and taking cases to the Supreme Court. Another (SCLC) takes a moral/religious approach that conducts campaigns of nonviolent resistance to break unjust laws and suffer the consequences, legal and otherwise. But the main goal is to stir the conscience of those who commit acts of hatred and brutality against them. A third (SNCC) follows the moral/religious approach of SCLC, but sees it as only partially effective in stirring up the conscience of those who uphold unjust laws, and not very effective at all in bringing people together in a true a community who could hold their heads high because they were rooted in their own communities and their own struggles for dignity and justice. This third approach looks to other means to dissuade the more hardened and violent advocates of segregation from, indirectly, becoming emboldened by nonviolent resistance, reserving the right to defend their communities when necessary.

By understanding the philosophical foundations for these methods, you can better understand how to argue for the outcomes that your factions most supports, based on the victory table for your faction that your faction leader holds, and how best to anticipate the ways in which other factions will argue for other outcomes and argue against some of those you advocate. You can also begin to see areas of agreement and ways to forge agreements between factions.

The philosophical foundations of faction positions and methods are not just of historical relevance. They are methods which were effective in the past, but which may be effective in the present and future as well. Any minority group can find its rights being denied by the majority, and the methods represented by these factions, together with the reasons, world views, principles and other philosophical foundations for them, can be used by people struggling against one or another form of oppression today. Those who seek to affect government policy with direct action—from unjust wars to the treatment of animals—must confront similar questions of what means are appropriate and effective to achieve any given ends.

1) Description of the Game Modules:

The Struggle for Civil Rights has been divided into several modules: two main modules and one introductory module. The two main modules, *Dorchester, 1963* and *Memphis, 1966*, are designed to be played for three-and-a-half weeks. The *Highlander Folk School* module is a one-and-a-half-week, preparatory/warm up module involving all of the students in a class, serving to "break the ice" and set the tone for the game(s). It should be conducted first; followed by either of the main modules, if only one is being played, or by both if both are being played. So, classes which only play one of the main modules will be devoting five weeks of their course to the game. Classes which play both main modules will be devoting eight-and-a-half weeks of their course to the game (the Highlander module does not need to be repeated for the second module).

1963 is significant for several reasons. While the NAACP had worked with Dr. Martin Luther King, Jr. and the Montgomery Improvement Association (MIA) during the Montgomery Bus Boycott, the NAACP had continued its legal approach to fighting segregation. They had been successful, each working a distinct approach to combating segregation, both together in the same protest. But Dr. King and others were not content to work under the leadership of the NAACP. Dr. King and other leaders of the MIA joined with members of the African-American religious community throughout the South and formed the SCLC with an aim to promote nonviolent resistance in future struggles. Their approach was distinct and equally valuable, even if some in the NAACP did not think it was helpful to the Movement. SNCC formed after the sit-in movement, which had not been directed by either NAACP or SCLC, though its methods resembled those of SCLC to a degree. But during the Albany protests (1961-62), these groups and other local groups found it difficult to work together. While there was some cooperation, there were philosophical differences, as well as economic and age differences in the members of the factions. Dr. King later felt that protests had been too general and would have been more effective by targeting specific laws and practices. When the results of the protests turned out not to have the kind of efficacy that had been sought, the Movement was on the verge of stagnating in its ability to contend with segregationists and the Jim Crow system of the South.

1966 is also significant for similar reasons. While there had been successes, including the passage of civil rights legislation, there was also increasing dissent, within the Civil Rights community, about the appropriate means for affecting meaningful change. Dr. King saw a need for SCLC to focus on more than the South of the United States, and also give voice to the plight of the poor generally and to the question of the moral worth of the war in Vietnam; positions with which some in SCLC and many in NAACP did not agree. Some in SNCC saw the results of nonviolent protests, including the bombing at a church in Birmingham, and the brutality at Selma, as evidence that nonviolence may be indirectly encouraging some hardened segregationists to react violently. They still believed that nonviolent tension could bring about change in the hearts of some, but not all, and it might not be able to generate the kind of friendships and true community that Dr. King and others saw it creating. They began to use the rhetoric of black power to express the dignity and strength of protesters conducting nonviolent campaigns, as well as their right to protect themselves and their loved ones as they carried on such protests. They began to see the NAACP, who firmly disapproved of such rhetoric, as far too eager to placate white politicians, and see SCLC as leaning in that direction as well. Again, the Movement was experiencing contentious forces that could rip it apart when James Meredith was shot and the leaders of the groups came together to try to work out a way to carry on his March Against Fear, in his honor and despite their differences.

Both of these moments in the Civil Rights Movement were preceded by an institution which had worked to help people organize in the Labor Movement and had turned its attention to civil rights in 1954, and found people and leaders willing to participate in activities, including Rosa Parks and Dr. King: The Highlander Folk School. The game will use the *Highlander Folk School* setting as an introductory/warm-up module to either or both of the main modules

Highlander Folk School

The *Highlander Folk School* module is a one-and-a-half-week module which is designed to precede either or both of the main modules for the game. It is also designed to familiarize students with some of the challenges of dealing with civil rights and race-related issues respectfully. It is based historically on the Highlander Folk School (Monteagle, TN). The Highlander Folk School had been working with the labor movement for years during the Depression and the War years, before they turned their full attention in 1954 to desegregation and civil rights, anticipating *Brown v. Board of Education* later in 1954. Their approach was to bring people together in an informal, relaxed setting to help discussions become more open, more respectful, and more likely to generate mutual understanding and the courage to take action against injustice and suffering, based on that understanding.

Dorchester, 1963

In this game module, characters will take up the struggle for nonviolent tension. In his "Letter from Birmingham Jail," Dr. King described nonviolent tension as part of a program of direct action which aimed to generate the kind of constructive tension that encourages moral growth. In the setting of the church at Dorchester Center, located near Midway, GA. January 10-12, 1963, characters will be considering more recent civil rights efforts, such as the activities in Albany, GA, (1961-1962, which many felt were not as helpful for the movement as they would have liked), as well as some of the early activities, such as the Bus Boycott in Montgomery.

Which kinds of activities should be focused on now? There have been sit-ins; there have been Freedom Rides. How do we best work to regain momentum in the struggle against the Jim Crow segregation of the South? Who do we look to for help? How do we direct our time, our financial resources, and the lives of the people who work for our organizations? The national leaders are trying to decide if the next major protest will be in Birmingham, Alabama, though some think that is dangerous and prefer protests in Louisville, KY. Each faction will have certain objectives that it wants to advance. Wildcard characters will also have objectives, some of which coincide with those of the factions, but some of which are more unique. Formal presentations and rebuttals will, no doubt, bring up what each character sees as the successes and failures of the past, and how they should inform plans for the future.

Memphis, 1966
In this game module, characters will take up the struggle for cultural pride, political power and progress toward more effective citizenship. These meetings are located in Memphis, Tennessee at the church of Rev. James Lawson, and will bring national leaders together on behalf of James Meredith, who has just been shot (June 6th) at the beginning of his March Against Fear from Memphis to Jackson, to discuss plans for continuing his March and related matters. There are divisions between members of the three factions about the wisdom of a Northern campaign, and also divisions regarding the means of future campaigns: should they always be nonviolent, should they welcome involvement with those who do not live by strictly nonviolent action? How should the movement respond to poverty, to the war in Vietnam? Which is the best strategy for civil rights? Litigation and lobbying? Community organizing with an eye toward majority rule in mostly-black areas? Or continue trying to awaken America's conscience?

2) Game Characters

Each student will learn about the ideas, goals and methods which clashed in this historically based game by 'playing' a character which is fictional, but often has the characteristics of at least one person who distinguished himself, or herself, during the Civil Rights Movement. In many cases, the biographies and victory objectives of a character resemble similar characteristics of more than one real person, and this has been done to emphasize the fact that no one is 'playing' an actual person who worked in the Movement.

While students will be playing their character role during the *Highlander Folk School* module, they will not be voting on any victory objectives. Instead, they will vote on which topics they would like to hear lectures about and talk about more, as part of a training experience at Highlander for future civil rights work. In the two main modules, *Dorchester 1963* and *Memphis 1966*, they will be following the information on the **character role sheet** that the gamemaster has given them with particular attention to the victory table for their faction (held by their faction leader), the grounding question of the game, and other clues and suggestions about the victory objectives of their factions. Wildcard characters will have more individualized victory objectives.

In general, there are two kinds of characters: those in factions (NAACP, SCLC and SNCC) and those who are not in factions: the Wildcards. Each faction consists, more specifically, of advisors and staffers, representatives of their organizations, who are to discuss the main question at the meeting, along with secondary questions, in ways that agree with the national leadership of their organizations. The decisions made by these representatives will influence the choices that the national leaders will have before them, and in many ways, these deliberations will be the "first round" of deliberations, since the national staffers, while expected to think for themselves, also have a good sense of the priorities and views of their organizations' national leaders. They are 'laying the groundwork' for the national leaders of those organizations who will meet at a later time to formalize whatever proposals are agreed upon.

All characters are dedicated to the Civil Rights Movement, despite differences in their understanding of how that movement should direct itself. There are no characters who are segregationists, white supremacists, or officials of local, state or federal governments. The game, then, focuses primarily on the **struggles *within* the Civil Rights Movement**, and only secondarily on the struggles with segregationists and white supremacists. Because there is some agreement in the overall goals of the Movement, and because it would be helpful to have something of a united front, the national leaders have asked that all of the main outcomes agreed to at the meeting be approved by a 60% majority of all voting characters.

Wildcard Characters (Indeterminants)

As mentioned, factions will also need to work with the wildcard characters who are not part of any formal faction. These characters have been invited to participate in the deliberations by the national leaders of the three organizations. They are important voices in the Civil Rights community. More importantly for the game, they have votes in the decision on which outcomes will be pursued, so factions will need to make appeals to them for their votes to try to garner the necessary support for the outcomes their faction wants to see approved. Each wildcard will prepare a formal presentation which will bring up aspects of the Civil Rights Movement that they feel should be considered in light of answering the main question for that game module (see above), and the gamemaster will discuss plans for their presentations with each wildcard, individually. Their views will often dovetail with the views of one or another faction, regarding the outcomes being voted on. Each wildcard will also do a second presentation, or two rebuttals (gamemasters discretion), responding to elements of the proposed-outcomes as is fitting for their character. Wildcard characters should study the material about the factions and their philosophical positions, as well as ask members of the factions questions, to better gauge common interests and areas of agreement.

Descriptions of the Factions

(Shot gun watch after firebomb threat at community center, 1964, © 1976 Matt Herron/Take Stock / The Image Works)

There are three factions in both main modules:
1) The NAACP
2) The SCLC
3) The SNCC

The **NAACP faction** is composed of advisers and staff members acting as the representatives of the National Association for the Advancement of Colored People. The NAACP was formed by a number of concerned, European-American leaders in 1910. They aimed to work against the disenfranchisement of African-American voting rights that was in full swing in Southern states, as well as fight against other injustices and crimes, such as discrimination, the 'separate, but equal' polities, rioting and lynching. The early NAACP gained additional vigor when it merged with many of the members of the Niagara Movement, most prominently, W.E.B. DuBois. In addition to working for anti-lynching legislation, the NAACP directed energies to publicizing injustices and atrocities as well as mounting a highly organized, and eventually well-financed legal challenge to various aspects of the unjust, Jim Crow system of segregation.

The faction believes that the Civil Rights Movement has made great strides by the careful process of challenging local and state segregation laws in the courts and appealing decisions up to the Supreme Court. Members of the faction are proud that their organization has been able to raise funds and carry on activities for years. They believe that the legal approach, while slow, is the best and most steady kind of progress in ending segregation. They see other activities, generally, as taking time and resources away from the legal approach. While they can appreciate some nonviolent activities, such as boycotts and marches, and while they have participated in such protests, they do not see the wisdom in protests which are geared to provoke a violent response from the larger community. Such protests will only turn people away from the movement, sap the resources of organizations such as the NAACP, dilute the work of the Movement generally, and get a lot of African-Americans hurt or killed in the process. Experience has shown them that the decisions of the Supreme Court, as well as the legislation of the federal government are the best tools for dealing constructively with the injustices of the past and establishing the foundation for greater freedom and equality in the future.

The **SCLC faction** is composed of advisors and staff members acting as representatives of the Southern Christian Leadership Conference. This organization was formed in 1957 in the wake of the successful Montgomery Bus Boycott, as other groups across the South began bus boycotts of their own. In January of 1957, members of the Montgomery Improvement Association (MIA) met with representatives of other groups with the hope of working together in a larger civil rights organization for the South. At the January meeting in Atlanta, they took the name, the Southern Leadership Conference on Transportation and Nonviolent Integration, but a month later at another meeting in New Orleans the name became Southern Leadership Conference, which was finally changed to the Southern Christian Leadership Conference (SCLC) at a third conference later that year in Atlanta.

The aim was to apply nonviolent methods of protest to large numbers of people in the hope of changing not just the customs of segregation, but the attitudes and ideas which fostered those customs. The larger goals of SCLC paralleled those of the NAACP, in that they wanted to help improve the economic, social and political realities of African-Americans generally, but the membership and leadership of SCLC came from the Black Church. Voter registration was a part of their efforts, but so was the kind of mass action that would not only attract attention to problems and injustices that the European-American community would have rather overlooked, but also reach out to members of the European-American community to encourage them to question their usual ways of thinking and behaving. SCLC planned and took part in boycotts and marches, as well as voter registration drives. They also took over administration of the Citizenship School program that the Highlander Folk School had started. This program helped teach African-Americans to read and write, not only so that they could register to vote, but also so that they could fill out job applications and personal checks, among other things.

Because its membership was so much a part of the Black Church, SCLC would call on church-going African-Americans to participate in various activities, as well as keep in contact with the community through church meetings. This gave them resources with which other organizations were not as closely connected. The style of leadership in SCLC also duplicated the often top-down kind of authority that existed in black churches. Frequently, meetings to discuss mass actions would take place in church basements, and the singing of religious songs and freedom songs would be a large part of the meeting itself. The songs would help ease the fears of people who knew that their participation in such protests could affect their jobs, their lives, and the lives of their loved ones.

SCLC's activities aimed at fostering a beloved community in which people who were formerly enemies or strangers would become friends and neighbors. Their methods differed from the more legal and legislative approach of the NAACP, but they acted as another front in the battle against injustice; another way to carry on the struggle.

The **SNCC faction** is composed of advisers and staff members acting as representatives of the Student Nonviolent Coordinating Committee. In the wake of the sit-ins that began in Greensboro in early 1960, civil rights leaders saw the possibility of young people becoming more active in the movement. Ella Baker, the organizer who had worked in the NAACP and more recently in SCLC as the executive secretary lobbied for a conference of student leaders, at which they could meet, share stories, and discuss goals and tactics. She modeled it on the *Highlander Folk School* meeting for young activists, held in the early Spring, but wanted to get more people involved from a wider array of groups. The conference was held in April of 1960 at Shaw University in Raleigh, North Carolina and brought together about three hundred students. Baker had been critical of the top-down style of leadership at SCLC, and wanted the students to have a more grassroots, bottom-up approach to leadership.

During the conference, students decided that though they'd been supported by a grant from SCLC, they needed to set up their own group, the Student Nonviolent Coordinating Committee, which would plan and organize sit-ins and other nonviolent protest activities. So, in April of 1960, SNCC was born, with Marion Barry serving as its first chairman.

The SNCC faction leans toward the views of SCLC on some issues, particularly during the Dorchester 1963 module. SNCC has been on the front lines of recent protests, including the sit-ins and some of the freedom rides. But in addition to putting themselves in harm's way as part of a nonviolent effort to change the hearts of others, they see these protests as a demonstration of being better than the segregationists who are lashing out at them. Generally,

SNCC has a greater commitment than NAACP and SCLC to grassroots organizing and community organization. They see themselves as proud and uncompromising black advocates for political and economic self-determination in their own communities. While they feel armed, self-defense groups, such as the Deacons for Defense and Justice, should be part of the movement, SNCC members themselves are committed to not taking up arms. They are not advocating riots or violent protests, but will also not tone down protests just because it makes others uncomfortable. They act from a demand for respect and dignity for people at the community level, and advocate grass-roots/local leadership in protests; not merely leadership from organizations far away without direct knowledge and contact in local communities.

By 1966, they are very concerned that the appearance of nonviolence in protesters may be giving some segregationists the wrong message: because it resembled the way African-Americans had been expected to defer to the authority of European-Americans in the past, it may give some people renewed energy to strike out at that nonviolent behavior. They are aware that some other people in the Civil Rights Movement see their rhetoric, affirming what they see as a more positive and realistic expression of dignity and black power, as unnecessary and unwise. They are also aware that the media often wrongly associates them with advocates of violent revolution. Nevertheless, they keep their call for dignity and respect nonviolent, while refusing to water-down their characterizations of the realities working against local communities that try to run their own businesses and stand up against the police brutality and mob violence that is still directed against them. So they are not always in agreement with SCLC or NAACP on certain issues.

3) Goals for the Game and 'Winning'

There are several goals for the game; some are directed at the participants in their roles and some are directed at the participants as students. A college-level, academic game is part of a course in which students are expected to develop specific skills and/or mastery of subject matter. So the ideas at the heart of debates within the Civil Rights community, as well as the history of events that form the context of those debates, the religious and philosophical influences, the economic, political and social realities, all form the subject matter that students are meant to learn by playing the game. They are also meant to develop their skill at public speaking, deliberation and writing papers.

As participants in their historically-situated roles, however, the goals take the form of achieving specific victory objectives; the main goal being to achieve one's victory objectives more completely than other characters. Characters in factions have victory charts which assign positive and negative point values for the various outcomes that participants will debate and, eventually, vote for or against. Characters in factions, for the most part, vote together, though there are exceptions that the gamemaster can allow.

<u>If a victory objective is approved</u> (by 60% in the case of primary outcome decisions, 50% in the case of secondary outcomes), <u>each fraction earns the position or negative victory points</u>. The Gamemaster knows the exact point numbers, and keeps track of that as decisions are made throughout the game.

Students, like participants in historical events, are not aware of the absolute value of their actions; they are only aware of the relative value of various outcomes, as specified on the Victory Tables; pp 12-14. For each outcome, the Victory Table for each student's faction will give one of three (3) designations: **Ideal, Acceptable, or Unsatisfactory**. **Ideal** means that the outcome is of highest importance for that particular category, from the point of view of that faction. **Acceptable** means that the outcome is a good outcome and welcome, though it is not as important as an Ideal outcome, from the point of view of that faction. **Unsatisfactory** means that the outcome may be helpful to some degree, but it takes time, attention and resources away from outcomes that are of greater importance, from the point of view of that faction. Obviously, factions will not always agree about which outcomes are Ideal, Acceptable and Unsatisfactory. In a perfect world, the Movement could advance many or all outcomes, but with limited resources, and with differences in their philosophical positions, each faction will try to achieve their Ideal outcomes and avoid any Unsatisfactory ones.

Only the game master will know the absolute point values of the outcomes, but the three designations give the students some direction in what to argue for or against, as well as their philosophical positions and character descriptions. Point totals can also be affected by other factors: the essay context from the Highlander Folk School module, and also points that factions "give up" to earn the vote of some of the wildcards, or earn by helping a wildcard. Since each faction does not know their point total at anytime, nor do they know the point total of other factions, they will have to ask the GM if they have points to "give up" to earn a wildcard vote, and will have to listen carefully to the arguments in faction presentations to gauge the extent to which other factions support or oppose the various outcomes they most want to achieve.

Winning the Game

(onlookers, Selma to Montgomery March, 1965, © 1976 Matt Herron/Take Stock / The Image Works)

The faction with the highest number of points by the end of the game "wins" the game and those students may be rewarded with a victory bonus, a small grade-bonus added to their grade for participation in the game, at the gamemaster's discretion. The victory bonus gives students added incentive to apply themselves in their discussions and presentations. Characters who are wildcards do not use the victory charts, but have specific victory goals that they are trying to advance. In some cases, their support will cost, or gain, victory points for the faction that works with them. Wildcards will work with the gamemaster to better understand the conditions under which they will be judged to have met their victory objectives, but generally speaking, they do not have to "out do" anyone else, but just get a specific outcome accepted by the members of the meeting.

Special Victory Bonus (also at the gamemaster's discretion)
If, by the end of the game, the point totals for the three main factions are within 4 points of each other, all game participants (faction members and wildcards) **will earn a ½ victory bonus, on top of any other bonus they have earned**. This special victory bonus reinforces the aim of the national leaders who believe that the success of upcoming protests will be much greater if their representatives can arrive at a strategy which satisfies all of the main factions.

Resource Points and Victory Points
Each faction will have a set number of Resource Points at the beginning of the module. Resource Points represent the resources (money, volunteers, expertise, etc…) that each faction has and can use to try to win the support of Wildcards for various outcomes. A faction may offer a Resource Point to a Wildcard who needs those resources to set up a project that is very important to that character. The faction cannot use a Resource Point to set up a project that goes against the principles of that faction, however. Also, the gamemaster must see and approve a written agreement between the Wildcard and the faction before a vote is taken in which a Wildcard is agreeing to vote a particular way after receiving a Resource Point.

In other words, if the faction is careful, they can 'spend' a Resource Point to enable a project that is not antithetical to their principles, as well as obtain a vote that could help pass a game outcome that grants them several Victory Points and moves their overall goals forward.

Each faction will have a Victory Chart which outlines their Resource Points and states the designations of relative worth (**Ideal, Acceptable or Unsatisfactory**) of each outcome. There can be only one Primary Form of Protest outcome, and, when it is passed by 60%, points will be awarded and kept confidential by the GM. Up to three Secondary Form of Protest outcomes may be passed, with merely a 50% vote, but the Victory Point values for the Secondary Form of Protest outcomes are cut in half. The following chart lists the outcomes; faction leaders have the values for their faction. The GM may suggest how each faction is doing, as the game progresses, by giving them a **Reaction Call** from that faction's national headquarters, which will indicate how the national leaders feel about the outcomes.

Dorchester Victory Table (sample, GM will give each faction member their victory table)

	NAACP	SCLC	SNCC
<u>Initial</u> **Resource Points**	?	?	?

    (Resource Points become Victory Points if unused)

<u>Relative Value</u> by Outcome (Ideal, Acceptable or Unsatisfactory):

Next Protest Site

	NAACP	SCLC	SNCC
Next major civil rights activities carried out in Birmingham, Alabama (nonviolent protests)	?	?	?
Next major civil rights activities carried out in Lousiville, KY (civil rights bill, integr. neighborhoods)	?	?	?

Forms of Protest (secondary forms of protest earn ½ point totals)
(there should be 1 primary and at most 3 secondary)

	NAACP	SCLC	SNCC
Primary focus of protest will be establishment of freedom/citizenship schools in AL	?	?	?
Primary focus of protest will be door to door voter registration in AL	?	?	?
Primary focus of protest will be court challenges to unfair voter registration laws and practices	?	?	?
Primary focus of protest will be nonviolent marches of symbolic import to pressure for integration and friendship	?	?	?
Primary focus of protest will be boycotts and selective buying campaigns to pressure for desegregation	?	?	?
Primary focus of protest will be nonviolent marches to publicize civil rights and voting rights bills	?	?	?
Primary focus of protest will be sit-ins, swim-ins and other similar nonviolent means to pressure for desegregation	?	?	?

Protest Leadership

	NAACP	SCLC	SNCC
Primary leaders of all organizations involved will lead and participate in the protest activities (Wilkins, King, Lewis)	?	?	?
Protests will be led by secondary leaders so that primary leaders can raise funds and sustain operations elsewhere	?	?	?
Protests will be led by local Civil Rights leaders (esp. Rev. Shuttlesworth) with the help of secondary leaders of the organizations	?	?	?

Memphis Victory Table (sample, GM will give each faction member their victory table)

	NAACP	SCLC	SNCC
Initial **Resource Points**	?	?	?

(Resource Points become Victory Points if unused)

Relative Value by Outcome (Ideal, Acceptable or Unsatisfactory):
Forms of Protest (secondary forms of protest earn ½ point totals)
(there should be 1 primary and at most 3 secondary)
(the first three forms of protest are mutually exclusive and should be considered at the same time)

	NAACP	SCLC	SNCC
Primary focus will be the March Against Fear itself, but carried on with the armed, Deacons for Defense and Justice	?	?	?
Primary focus will be the March Against Fear itself, but carried on with participants permitted to carry firearms for protection	?	?	?
Primary focus will be the March Against Fear itself, while national leaders use it to draw attention to civil rights legislation	?	?	?
- - - - - - - - - - -
Primary focus of protest will be door to door voter registration and est. freedom schools in MS and TN, lengthen route	?	?	?
Primary focus of protest will be to demand that the Real Estate Associations in TN and MS support, rather than discourage, Black family movement into newly integrated neighborhoods.	?	?	?
Primary focus of protest will be sit-ins, boycotts in towns on the route to put attention on hiring practices, availability of doctors, lawyers, and banks for Black-Americans there	?	?	?
Primary focus of protest will be opposition to tax-exempt status for all-White, private schools being est. in the South	?	?	?
Primary focus of protest will be generating support for a Northern campaign against poverty and injustice in cities such as Chicago and New York	?	?	?
Primary focus of protest will be publicity, and allocating funds, for bringing Black students and community leaders from the North, to work on Civil Rights organizing in MS and TN	?	?	?
Primary focus of protest will be raising funds for college scholarships for needy black students in TN and MS.	?	?	?

Victory Point Distributions by Outcome (for Memphis, continued):

Protest Leadership (these outcomes are mutually exclusive and should be considered at the same time)

Primary leaders of all organizations involved will lead and participate in the March (Wilkins, King, Carmichael)	?	?	?
Protests will be led by secondary leaders so that primary leaders can raise funds and sustain operations elsewhere	?	?	?

March Participation (these outcomes are mutually exclusive and should be considered at the same time)

Participation open to all members of civil rights organizations and to local people along the March route	?	?	?
Participation <u>only</u> open to Black-American members of civil rights organizations and Black-American people along the March route	?	?	?

4) Structure of Debates and Votes on Outcomes

The factions of *The Struggle for Civil Rights* are understood to be prominent members of the Civil Rights community, but not the national leaders of their respective groups. The game assumes that the national leaders several civil rights groups have sent some of their most trusted advisers and staff people to do "advance" work—lay the foundation for a meeting to determine the direction of protest activities in the near future, which they mean to conduct in concert with other civil rights groups. The game participants take on these advisor/staffer roles and attempt to work out agreements ahead of the meeting of the national leaders in mid-January, 1963.

Students begin by getting familiar with their character roles, hearing lectures on various aspects of the civil rights movement and setting up the framework of the game during the Highlander Folk School module.

Highlander Folk School

The first main module played will be preceded by the *Highlander Folk School* module. On the first day, the wildcard character Bernice Lewis will do her presentation after leading the group in a freedom song. She will lead the group in freedom songs at the beginning of each day of the game in all modules. Students, in character, will also discuss which lecture topics (provided by the gamemaster) they can choose from, and will vote on the topics to be heard over the next two classes.

On the second day of *Highlander*, the gamemaster (as topic expert) will lecture on one or more of the chosen topics, and also discuss facts about the Highlander Folk School and both the Labor and Civil Rights Movement. Students will draft a tentative *Presentation Schedule* to be finalized at the next class meeting.

On the third and final day of *Highlander*, the gamemaster (as topic expert) will lecture on one more of the chosen topics, and also discuss facts about the Highlander Folk School and both the Labor and Civil Rights Movement. Students will finalize the *Presentation Schedule* and make it available to the gamemaster to distribute (electronically or otherwise) to all game participants. In the remaining time, the gamemaster will lead all participants in a group activity. Finally, the gamemaster will remind the students about the **Impolite/Offensive Behavior and Language Penalty** and the **Spirit of Highlander Award**.

Impolite/Offensive Behavior and Language Penalty

To encourage passionate but polite discussions, debates and deliberations, the gamemaster will give a student a **yellow, warning card**, if their words and/or behavior cross the line from focused on ideas, methods and plans to the people who have advocated for those ideas, methods and plans. This can include rude or offensive words, gestures or behavior. The second time it happens, that student will receive a **red, violation card and his or her faction will lose a victory point**. Further violations from anyone in that faction (regardless of whether or not it is their first time) will also result in the one victory point penalty. The gamemaster will continue this practice into the main modules of the game.

Spirit of Highlander Award

To encourage students to understand the history and methodology of Highlander, the gamemaster will require all participants to compose a **short (roughly 3 pg) essay** on five things about the history and methodology of Highlander Folk School which could help the civil rights struggle, due shortly after the *Highlander Folk School* module. Each student will write their essay from the point of view of their character, and will include details about the history of Highlander as well as the reasoning behind the way Highlander conducted its workshops. The gamemaster will grade the essays and (**Gamemaster's discretion**) average them with the other written work for the game, but will also rank the essays. If a student receives a red violation card during the game, his or her position in the rankings will drop by one. At the end of the game (at the end of the last module played), the gamemaster will reveal who has won the Spirit of Highlander Award, who is at the top of the rankings, and that character will earn a **victory bonus** (if a wildcard) **or 2 victory points for his or her faction** (if a faction member). (**Gamemaster's discretion**)

After the *Highlander Folk School* module, one or the other of the main modules will begin. The *Presentation Schedule* will have already been established. Since faction members know the views of the national leaders, and of their organizations generally, and since they are in contact with those leaders frequently by phone or fax, they have been trusted to work out disagreements and try to forge alliances with other groups so that the upcoming protests will be more effective at advancing the goals of the Movement. Various groups have attempted to work together in the past, but the results have not always been successful. There have been disagreements about the means used in the protests, disagreements about the pace of various activities, and disagreements about where the funds will come from to pay for the various costs associated with these activities (food and lodging requirements for marchers, bail money, etc…).

But the national leaders have urged their representatives to forge compromises and work toward consensus.

In fact, to encourage that push for consensus, they have required that the main outcomes which are passed by the group members must have at least 60% support of the voting members present.

Dorchester 1963: The Struggle for Nonviolent Tension: Where, How and Who Will Lead?

There are three main outcomes for *Dorchester 1963* are:

1) the Next Protest Site outcome
2) the Primary Form of Protest outcome
3) the Protest Leadership outcome

The game participants consider making the Next Protest Site at Birmingham, AL, but the NAACP faction is in favor of another site: Louisville, KY. So the first debate will focus on which location for carrying out upcoming Civil Rights protests. This debate needs to occur first and will shape subsequent decisions.

Furthermore, in an effort to be effective, the national leaders have required that one of the protest activity outcomes be voted on as the designated Primary Form of Protest outcome for the upcoming protest activities. No more than three of the remaining outcomes can be agreed on as Secondary Outcomes, because there is not enough time and resources to do everything that each faction wants. Efforts must be concentrated and tough decisions must be made. In practice, at the meetings, this will work by having debates on each of the Forms of Protest outcomes separately. After each debate, participants will vote on whether to make that Form of Protest the Primary one for the upcoming event. If a Form of Protest outcome does not meet the 60% requirement, it can be reconsidered, at any later time, as a Secondary Form of Protest with only a 50% requirement.

Faction leaders have the responsibility to consult with their faction members, with wildcards, and with each other to determine on which days each Form of Protest Outcome will be debated and voted on. If there are disagreements about the order which cannot be resolved in a timely fashion, the presiding officer will have authority to make a final decision.

Finally, one of three outcomes will be debated and voted on to determine the Protest Leadership outcome. Some participants feel it is important that the national leaders take an active role in the protests themselves. Others believe that the protest will not have the endurance necessary if the national leaders, many of whom are responsible for raising and efficiently distributing funds, are overly occupied with hands-on protest activities and/or serving time in jail. They feel that secondary leaders can carry out the protests. Still others will argue that local leaders who best know the area, people and officials should lead the protests.

Memphis 1966: The Struggle for Black Power:
How, Who Will Lead, and Who Will Participate?

There are also three main outcomes for *Memphis 1966*:

1) the Primary Form of Protest outcome
2) the Protest Leadership outcome
3) the March Participation outcome

As in the *Dorchester 1963* module, the national leaders, for *Memphis 1966*, have required that one of the protest activity outcomes be voted on as the designated Primary Form of Protest outcome for the upcoming protest activities. No more than two of the remaining outcomes can be agreed on as Secondary Outcomes, because there is not enough time and resources to do everything that each faction wants. In practice, at the meetings, this will work by having debates on each of the Forms of Protest outcomes separately. The first three Form of Protest outcomes are mutually exclusive, however, and should be debated and voted on, on the same day. After each debate, participants will vote on whether to make that Form of Protest the Primary one for the upcoming event. If a Form of Protest outcome does not meet the 60% requirement, it can be reconsidered, at any later time, as a Secondary Form of Protest with only a 50% requirement.

Faction leaders have the responsibility to consult with their faction members, with wildcards, and with each other to determine on which days each Form of Protest Outcome will be debated and voted on. They do not have to be voted on in the order they are listed for the Memphis Victory Tables. If there are disagreements about the order which cannot be resolved in a timely fashion, the presiding officer will have authority to make a final decision.

One of two outcomes will be debated and voted on to determine the Protest Leadership outcome. Some participants feel it is important that the national leaders take an active role in the protests themselves. Others believe that the protest will not have the endurance necessary if the national leaders, many of whom are responsible for raising and efficiently distributing funds, are overly occupied with hands-on protest activities and/or serving time in jail. They feel that secondary leaders can carry out the protests. The two Protest Leadership outcomes are mutually exclusive and should be debated and voted on, on the same day.

Finally, there is division as to who the participants of the March should be. Some argue that the participants should be members of the various civil rights organizations, as well as local people. Others believe that it will send a stronger and more positive message to the Black community in Tennessee and Mississippi if participation is limited to African-Americans. Those two outcomes for March Participation are mutually exclusive and should be debated and voted on, on the same day.

5) Game Format and Requirements for Participants

In order to earn points for decisions which support their faction's victory objectives, faction members will give presentations and do rebuttals during the game, which will be graded by the gamemaster as part of their overall grade for the academic game. Wildcards will have individual victory objectives and their presentations and rebuttals will be tailored toward advancing those objectives, in consultation with the gamemaster.

Each participant will do either two formal presentations (10 min. ea.), or one formal presentation (10 min.) and one or two rebuttal presentations (2-5 min. each), in each of the two main modules. The gamemaster will help determine how many formal presentations will work given time constraints and the number of participants. These presentations will be written out before each presentation is made, and submitted to the gamemaster. Presentations and rebuttals will be organized by the faction leaders, as part of the effort to make sure all voices are heard before votes are taken on the outcomes detailed in each faction's victory charts, though the character who is presiding over the meetings in each of the main modules (Rev. Jones, for *Dorchester*; and Mr. Robinson, for *Memphis*) may take *ad hoc* rebuttals if faction leaders agree. The victory charts for each faction are guided by the grounding questions for each of the two main modules:

The main grounding question for *Dorchester, 1963* is:
Should protests against segregation be conducted in Birmingham, and, if so, what kind of activities should protesters undertake, based on lessons learned over the last few years in Albany and elsewhere?

The main grounding question for *Memphis, 1966* is:
Should Meredith's March Against Fear be continued, and, if so, what kind of activities should accompany the march and what kinds of protection should be secured, based on lessons learned over the last few years in Birmingham, Selma and elsewhere?

Each faction leader will need to help his or her faction to develop an outline of the faction's positions on the various outcomes from their victory chart. Each faction should also decide who will defend or oppose the various outcomes on the victory chart, so that the dates for those presentations can be scheduled as soon as possible.

Faction leaders will work together to set up the *Presentation Schedule* which will include not only their own faction members, but all of the wildcards as well.

Presentations

These formal presentations should not only argue for aspects of each character's position, but should anticipate objections and attempt to deal with them. They should also make reference to facts, events, and experiences from the time period. Presenters must express the emotional connection that their character has to the goals and methods which are part of the outcomes being discussed and debated. Unless the gamemaster says otherwise, presentations should be **about**

ten minutes long, and the papers which are based on those presentations should be about five, double-spaced pages. <u>In addition to the first presentation, each participant should also do a second presentation, or one-two rebuttals (gamemasters discretion)</u>,

Rebuttals

Faction leaders will also organize some of the rebuttals for each formal presentation. Rebuttals will be shorter presentations which are directed at specific formal presentations. Many will take issue with the formal presentation, though others can offer support for that presentation. Unless the gamemaster says otherwise, rebuttals should be between three and five minutes in length, and the short papers which are based on those rebuttals should be two to three, double-spaced pages. Each character in the game will do two of these rebuttals, and faction leaders will be responsible for working out a schedule of the rebuttals as well as the formal presentations.

Organization of Class Meetings

Presiding Officer

The presentation schedule, as mentioned, will allot time for rebuttals to each of the factions and the wildcards, but individual students can request to do a rebuttal formally, in advance of that day, or by asking the Presiding Officer at the beginning of that day. In scheduling rebuttals, the Presiding Officer will make a good effort to allow the views of all factions and wildcards to be heard. He or she will also be award to time constraints.

In the *Dorchester, 1963* module, <u>the SCLC faction leader, Rev. Jones</u> holds the honorary position of presiding over the meetings. In the *Memphis, 1966* module, <u>the wildcard character, Philip Robinson</u> holds the honorary position as presiding officer.

Unless there is a collective decision to change this position, the presiding officer will call on each presenter and each character doing a rebuttal. The *presentation schedule* will be determined at the beginning of the module, but rebuttals will need to be formally requested. Characters will let the presiding officer know when they'd like to do a rebuttal, by the beginning of that session. It may be that more rebuttals are done after one presentation than after others. The presiding officer must make a great effort to be even-handed in trying to accommodate the requests of factional characters and wildcards alike. If the presiding officer is not being even-handed, he or she can be replaced by a majority vote of all game characters.

Beginning of Meetings

Each meeting will begin with a freedom song led by the wildcard character **Bernice Lewis**. Bernice feels strongly that the representatives at this meeting need to work together and set aside big personalities and agendas. She believes that the freedom songs are a force for fellowship and courage, and they will remind everyone of the difficulties that protesters have encountered in the past (since many sang the songs in not only in preparation for protest activities, but when they faced an uncertain future in prison). She was invited to the meeting, but has decided not to vote on any of the outcomes, but rather try to help everyone continue to see the need to work together.

After Mrs. Lewis leads everyone in a freedom song, one of the Minsters present will give a brief word of prayer. These prayers will not be long and will generally call on an all-powerful and just God to lend His Grace to that day's meeting.

The End of the Day Votes

At the end of most days, the characters will vote on one of the outcomes in the victory charts. The character's victory objectives, and their particular victory charts, as well as the way they have come to understand those objectives after hearing the presentations and rebuttals of their classmates' characters, will shape their votes. Factions will not have access to the victory charts for other factions. The national leaders want the representatives to work toward an agreement that **60%** of the characters approve, for the main outcomes. This will require working with wildcards and/or members of other factions. By requiring a two-thirds majority, the national leaders believe that there will be a greater sense of consensus and, hopefully, greater commitment to work together.

Dress Code

Since these meetings will take place in a church, the characters need to be wearing formal clothes. Hence, there will be a strict dress-code starting right after you have finished the *Highlander Folk School* module. Wear what you would wear to a place of worship. If this seems surprising, or disturbing, consider that students like yourselves, who went to work in African-American communities, often found out once they arrived that they would have to buy a suit to wear to most meetings because those meetings took place in churches. The local church was often the only place where people gathered on a regular basis. If you wanted to earn the respect and trust of people, who could be punished in various ways for working with civil rights organizers, it only made sense to respect their traditions by dressing properly in the church, and minding your manners. Your characters can break unjust laws, but not the dress code. The specifics of the dress code fall under the gamemaster's discretion.

Dorchester 1963 Schedule of Assignments and Class Activities

The schedule that follows assumes a class of up to twenty-five students. Larger classes may require more class sessions to allow all students to express complete their presentations.

Class	Student Assignment BEFORE class	Activity DURING class
(1)	Read Player's Handbook Introduction, Chps. 1-4 and Appendix 3	Highlander Module, Day 1: Bernice Lewis Presentation Choose lectures for next time
(2)	Read Appendix 1	Gamemaster (expert) lectures on one or more of the chosen topics Draft Presentation Schedule
(3)	Read Appendix 2	Gamemaster (expert) lectures on one or more of the chosen topics Finalize Presentation Schedule & Do **Group Activity**
(4)	Read Primary Reading Assignments (See Appendix 4) Reread Ch. 2 and 3	Begin *Dorchester 1963* module Begin presentations and debate for **Next Protest Site** Vote on **Next Protest Site**
(5) – (9)	Reread Ch. 2 and relevant sections of Appendix 2	Begin presentations and debate on the **Form of Protest** scheduled for today Vote on that **Form of Protest**
(10)	Reread Ch. 2 and relevant sections of Appendix 2	Begin presentations and debate on the **Protest Leadership** outcome **Post-Mortem** Discussion

Memphis 1966 Schedule of Assignments and Class Activities

The schedule that follows assumes a class of up to twenty-five students. Larger classes may require more class sessions to allow all students to express complete their presentations.

Class	Student Assignment BEFORE class	Activity DURING class
(1)	Read Player's Handbook Introduction, Chps. 1-4 and Appendix 3	Highlander Module, Day 1: Bernice Lewis Presentation Choose lectures for next time
(2)	Read Appendix 1	Gamemaster (expert) lectures on one or more of the chosen topics Draft Presentation Schedule
(3)	Read Appendix 2	Gamemaster (expert) lectures on one or more of the chosen topics. Finalize Presentation Schedule & Do **Group Activity**
(4)	Read Primary Reading Assignments (See Appendix 4) Reread Chps. 2 and 4	Begin *Memphis 1966* module *Begin presentations and debate for **Form of Protest** *Vote on **Form of Protest**
(5) – (7)	Reread Ch. 2 and relevant sections of Appendix 2	*Begin presentations and debate on the **Form of Protest** scheduled for today *Vote on that **Form of Protest**
(8)	Reread Ch. 2 and relevant sections of Appendix 2	*Begin presentations and debate on the **Protest Leadership** outcome
(9)	Reread Ch. 2 and relevant sections of Appendix 2	*Presentations and debate on **March Participation** outcome
(10)		**Post-Mortem** Discussion

Nonviolent Tension and Resistance

One of the central features of nonviolent resistance, whether it takes the form of marches, sit-ins or boycotts, is that while its initiatives have ethical and political import, they are carefully organized to make violence the least likely of consequences. To understand the reason for this, we need to understand the long-term goal of nonviolent resistance: communities of brotherhood, trust and mutual caring for one another. To achieve this, people living in the same location, who are either strangers or enemies, need to become friends. Friendship, however, cannot be forced. Efforts to have laws declared unconstitutional, while important and necessary in their own manner, cannot help people want to refrain from keeping those laws in effect. Enacting new laws, while important, cannot by itself make people want to follow those laws, and people who are in the habit of thinking of and acting a certain way toward people from another cultural group, will not break from those habits just because new legislation encourages them to do so.

The motivation for the "separate but equal" policy would remain in people's hearts if the laws were the only thing that changed. That policy (even if "separate" had really been "equal") implies an equality of conformism. As long as schools, bathrooms, and water fountains are the same, the policy asserts that it is permissible that some are reserved for one ethnic group and some for another. In other words, as long as the outward features of our lives are the same, we are equal to one another. As long as we behave properly, predictably, we are equal. But such conformity does not have a place for respecting differences between people. It does not encourage us to appreciate others as unique. Indeed, it stifles activities that veer away from the status quo.

Nonviolent resistance implies an equality of peers. It recognizes that people are different in many ways, but it also springs from the conviction that if confronted with intelligence and compassion, people can be persuaded to let go of their prejudices and to desire friendship which values people for who they uniquely are. As Dr. King argues in "Letter from Birmingham City Jail," direct action is a means for 'persuading' others to respect you as a peer:

> In these negotiating sessions certain promises were made by the merchants ....As the weeks and months unfolded we realized that we were the victims of a broken promise. The signs remained. So we had no alternative except that of preparing for direct action, whereby we would present our very bodies as a means of laying our case before the conscience of the local and national community (Martin Luther King, Jr., "Letter from Birmingham City Jail," in *A Testament of Hope*, p290-1)

Direct action, i.e. physical actions which put people at risk of being harmed or put in prison, were the means of persuasion, of "laying our case before" people who do not want to consider us their peers.

The short-term goal was genuine negotiation, as opposed to the sham negotiation Dr. King and others had to endure initially. Responding to the clergy who had criticized his actions in Birmingham, Dr. King responded:

> So the purpose of the direct action is to create a situation so crisis packed that it will inevitably open the door to negotiation. We, therefore, concur with you in your call for negotiation. Too long has our beloved Southland been bogged down in the tragic attempt to live in monologue rather than dialogue. (King, "Letter," p292)

A negotiation consisting of one side talking and the other listening is not based on an equality of peers. It is a monologue, as King asserts. But when an institution for genuine dialogue does not exist, he argues that direct action can find creative ways to initiate such dialogue. Indeed, they are not merely clever. By means of boycotts and sit-ins, they so stir the conscience of others that they create the opportunity for people to look beyond their habitual ways of regarding others as equal only if they share the same cultural and ethnic background, and instead, respect others as equal because of what makes them unique, culturally and historically.

If the activity undertaken is composed of offensive language and violent behavior, it will tend to make people afraid, and it is unlikely that such people will pay much attention to their conscience. The influence of the conscience will become drowned out by the fearful and angry reaction that many people will have to a violent act of protest. Instead, people who were strangers or enemies, will turn away from the message behind the protest and simply regard the activity as bad behavior and nothing more.

When the protest is nonviolent, people are challenged to think about their institutions differently, without being made afraid. Such a protest respects others enough to trust that they can be awakened in this manner. It does not seek to force others to behave in a certain way, through violence, fines or the threat of either. Rather, it confronts them so that they cannot pretend that there is not a problem, and then leaves space for their conscience to work. It attempts to persuade with actions that are unique and often unpredictable. But it does not directly or indirectly force others to comply: if the people around us are to become our friends, our good neighbors, they must take up our invitation freely.

The very invitation to become good neighbors, nevertheless, can be seen as hostile. Its goal is to change the community, so anyone comfortable with, or dedicated to preserving, the customs, values and laws of a community may feel threatened by such resistance, even when it stays nonviolent. This tension is inevitable; it must be expected to one degree or another. As Dr. King pointed out:

> I have earnestly opposed violent tension, but there is a type of constructive, nonviolent tension which is necessary for growth. Just as Socrates felt that it was necessary to create a tension in the mind so that individuals could rise from the bondage of myths and half-truths to the unfettered realm of creative analysis and objective appraisal, so must we see the need for nonviolent gadflies to create the kind of tension in society that will help men rise from the dark depths of prejudice and racism to the majestic heights of understanding and brotherhood. (King, "Letter," p291)

So, Dr. King understood that nonviolent resistance would entail nonviolent tension, and various activities from lunch-counter sit-ins, to freedom rides, to marches, were part of the effort to initiate that tension. It was dangerous and, from Dr. King's point of view, indispensable. It also created another kind of tension; the tension within the civil rights community. Over the years, some people began to question the worth of nonviolent resistance. Did it really stir up the conscience in all cases, or did it merely continue and reinforce a custom from the days of slavery that prohibited fighting back when someone of African descent was threatened or attacked by someone of European descent? How long can someone passively endure abuse before they act to remove the means of that abuse?

Dr. King, following Gandhi, would argue that nonviolent resistance is active, not passive. The tension and discontent of people in the African-American community cannot be wished away, but it does not have to become a catalyst for violence. He complained about the "bitterness and hatred" of some black nationalist groups whose rhetoric approached calls for violence. Instead of "letting out" such tension in unhelpful ways, Dr. King advocated that the community channel them into nonviolent activities designed to foster the tension necessary to press the civil rights movement forward. As he argued:

> The Negro has many pent-up resentments and latent frustrations, and he must release them. So let him march; let him make prayer pilgrimages to the city hall; let him go on freedom rides….So I have not said to my people: "Get rid of your discontent." Rather, I have tried to say that this normal and healthy discontent can be channeled into the creative outlet of nonviolent direct action. (King, "Letter," p297)

The struggle for nonviolent resistance is, then, a struggle to cultivate the kind of tension that will help all members of a community grow together. In the sense that African-Americans and European-Americans were not living "as" a community, nonviolent resistance is a means to creating community where only a façade of community existed before. It was controversial both within and outside the African-American community. As a guiding principle, it supported efforts to change the Jim Crow laws that had enforced Segregation, but it worked on people's motivations in a different manner, by trying to change their hearts. It understood the importance of actively opposing injustice, but also called for the discipline to channel that action intelligently, as well as passionately. Furthermore, while it was sophisticated in theory, it was also difficult in practice; there were no clear-cut answers regarding what kind of protest would be most effective, and which ones people would be most likely to join. The details were worked out by hard practice, by taking up the struggle for nonviolent tension.

Philosophical Positions of the Factions

National Association for the Advancement of Colored People (NAACP)

In its early days, the NAACP acted to raise awareness about atrocities committed against African-Americans, as well as advocate for equality wherever possible. They publicized lynchings and worked to get legislation outlawing lynching enacted. They also appealed to the federal government, including the president, on a variety of issues: e.g. opposing the segregation of the army by President Woodrow Wilson; advocating for African-American officers in the Army; arguing against a Supreme Court nominee who had a reputation for supporting legislation against the rights of African-Americans. But some of the greatest achievements of the NAACP were the result of a massive effort to fight prejudice and segregation by attacking the heart of the American system of government: the law.

One way this was advanced was by taking cases up through the courts to the Supreme Court, in the hopes that segregation laws would be overturned by the Court for violating one of the Civil War Amendments (13th-15th) These amendments were part of the legal fabric of our country. When the Union forces of the North had won the war and began the period known as Reconstruction, various measures were advocated to protest the rights of African-Americans, and the Civil War Amendments were the highest expression of that effort. In order to be readmitted to the Union, and ensure that Federal troops would be removed, formerly-Confederate states had to ratify one or more of these Amendments. It would have seemed that race would no longer be an issue that state and local legislatures could use to deny rights to African-American, Latino-Americans, Native-Americans and others.

As time passed, however, politicians in the South looked to the Supreme Court to undo the effectiveness of these Amendments and subsequent Civil Rights legislation (passed from 1866-1875). An 1883 ruling on a test case advanced against the 1875 Civil Rights Act began to unravel the intent and muscle of such legislation, and the infamous *Plessy v. Ferguson* ruling of 1898 began the assertion that "separate but equal" facilities and accommodations were permitted by the Civil War Amendments when states enacted such legislation. Justices argued that the Amendments were basically temporary measures to help out African-Americans just after slavery, but that the Amendments could not be taken to assert that people of different races should live together and work together.

Legal minds in the NAACP saw this judicial 'revision' of the Civil War Amendments for what it was: turning back the clock on Civil Rights. It was a bad reading of the Amendments, which the NAACP felt could be corrected if a more clear-headed Court were to take up these issues again. Just as test cases had been moved from lower courts to the Supreme Court to undo the intent of the Civil War Amendments, the NAACP would make a concerted effort to advance test cases of their own. Charles Hamilton Houston and Thurgood Marshall were two of the primary leaders, though there were others.

These efforts would take time and money. Finding cases to challenge the Black Codes and Jim Crow legislation was not easy; they needed to find cases in which segregation was the focus of the case and in which there were no other details that might distract justices. Once a case for found, money for lawyers and legal materials needed to be raised. These efforts were slowed during the Depression and War years, in part because it became more difficult to raise the necessary funds. Funds to bring in experts to testify to the educational and sociological effects of segregation were also needed to better make the case that the Jim Crow legislation acted against African-American and other minorities, it did not merely separate one race from another.

The strategy was to begin with graduate school admissions and win some rulings on cases in which people were denied admission to graduate schools, or asked to attend in some other state, on the basis of race. If they could win victories there, it would form the basis for a precedent against segregation laws and customs generally. The most significant plateau in this process was the *Brown v. Board of Education* cases in 1954, in which the Justices, ruling unanimously, overturned the "separate, but equal" doctrine and called for integration of public schools.

By taking the long, hard road of building precedents which could eventually be used to overturn Jim Crow legislation, the NAACP believed it could demonstrate that the highest law of the country, the Constitution, stood against segregation. If they could do that, Jim Crow legislation would have to crumble. The country would have to change the Constitution itself to legally continue segregation and that was unlikely given the requirements for amending the Constitution. By focusing on the law, the NAACP was appealing to an aspect of American democracy that was cherished by Americans from all parts of the country. It was part of the ideal of democracy in America that the law would not be a ruling from a king or dictator, but the will of the people legislating for themselves. The law would also be understood to protect those who were in the minority and not become a tyranny of the majority. On any issue, people might differ, but they would still respect the law and the rule of law. If that was the case, then establishing an understanding that the law did not allow for segregation was the most powerful action that could be taken by anyone or any institution to ensure the rights and dignity of African-Americans. It was not flashy; it was not fast. In the end, however, the legal effort to take cases to the Supreme Court would, they believed, bring the most lasting and effective change in race relations in the country.

In addition to court challenges, the NAACP also advanced Civil Rights legislation, including more federal legislation. While difficult because of the entrenched positions of some politicians, the NAACP applied pressure when and where they could. This involved lobbying politicians in Congress, and the President, and such efforts also required funds for travel and for publicizing the effects of segregation and prejudice to pressure politicians on important legislation. The NAACP was a large organization which realized that the prosperity of some African-Americans, if properly directed, could help pass legislation that would benefit all minorities in America. It involved careful planning and organization, and time, but they believed it would bring lasting change to the benefit of African-Americans and other minorities, so it was worth it.

Southern Christian Leadership Conference (SCLC)

The philosophical position of SCLC grows from an assertion of responsibility to fight injustice and a desire to foster true community, both of which have divine sanction. God calls on us to fight injustice no matter how difficult or inconvenient to us personally. But by fighting injustice, by fighting sin, we are not to fight the sinner, the person who has taken unjust actions against us. God is on our side in this fight, and will help us, but there will be set backs as well as victories, and we must find a way to persevere.

Dr. King articulates this position in many of his articles and speeches. He finds support from his Christian heritage: 1) from the African-American religious experience in which preachers play a role in the social aspects of people's lives, as well as in the more personal aspects; and 2) from the tradition of the Social Gospel in which it is understood that we cannot ignore the suffering and injustice around us to concentrate merely on our personal salvation, but must act to help those who are poor, who are hungry and who are being terrorized by people in their own country, in order to bring about a new kind of society, the beloved community, as King called it; the kingdom of God on earth.

Because this calling is directed at the sin and not the sinner, it looks to redeem the sinner from his or her errant ways. Segregation has engrained not only prejudice but a tolerance for, and tendency toward, violence and cruelty against African-Americans, but our actions must be directed toward rooting out that prejudice and that tendency, not at harming the people who have succumbed to them.

Therefore, the goal will not only be to change the laws and customs of segregation that have sustained and advanced a cruel and unjust way of life, but the establishment of an integrated community by nonviolent means. The goal of a beloved community is important, but it cannot be obtained by force. Nor can it be obtained merely by reasoning with those in power. Those in power, and the people who support them, are not living to their full potential as human beings. They have fallen into ways that are untrue, harmful and sinful. Arguing with them is important, but it will bear little fruit by itself. Working to change laws through legislation, or by appealing decisions to the Supreme Court, is a method with merit, but ultimately someone has to follow the new laws and uphold the Court's decisions. In the end, segregationists have the votes they need to stay in power and can influence who sits on the Supreme Court. In the end, laws are only as good as the people who live by them and enforce them, and the SCLC is dedicated to helping change the hearts of people whose ways and prejudices are deeply engrained.

At the center of this effort is an insight that Dr. King attributed to Gandhi: "unearned suffering is redemptive." Well constructed arguments may work on an intellectual level, but the minds and emotions of segregationists have been clouded. They still have a conscience, but it has been shielded and insulated over the years. The effort to change their hearts, to redeem the sinner, must break through that shield, and in many cases it can only happen when the shame that follows watching another's unearned suffering sinks deep into a person's thoughts and feelings. Intellectual arguments rarely bring on shame, especially on a large scale. But nonviolent action that is part of a carefully crafted campaign against unjust laws and practices can begin to stir up the conscience. When protesters are thwarted by cruelty and violence and refuse to respond in kind, but maintain their nonviolent protest, it calls on the better part in all people to respond with shame: shame for a society that has engendered such cruelty and violence and shame for our own actions when they fell into step with the aims of segregation.

This position is not merely a copying of Gandhi's principle, but has support in the New Testament, and in the central feature of the life of Jesus Christ. When Jesus says in Matthew, chapter five, that we are not to return "an eye for an eye" he means we are to do something that others will not expect. The segregationists will expect someone to return a violent attack with a violent response; an eye for an eye. Or, the segregationist may expect African-Americans to be frightened into submission and merely back down or run away from a fight. But Jesus said, when someone has struck you on one cheek, turn to him the other. He did not say "run away" nor did he say "hit back," nor even to "ask for pity," but to "turn to him the other cheek." I may run away to preserve myself; I may hit back to defend myself, and I may ask or cry for pity so someone else will help me; but in all three cases, I am doing these actions for my own benefit. I am also allowing those who oppose me to think only of themselves: if I run away, they think they are powerful; if I hit back, they think they are justified in their actions and can defend themselves; if I ask for pity, they think they are superior to me. Jesus says to avoid that those kinds of actions, and instead, do something that forces your opponent to genuinely encounter and engage you on the highest level. If someone wants to steal your shirt, give him your coat as well. If someone forces you to walk a mile, walk two. It may be more instinctual to hate someone who treats you with injustice and cruelty, but Jesus said to love such people, to love one's enemies. The meaning that Dr. King and others saw in this was that we are called to stand up to injustice, to segregation, and not back down. We are to allow ourselves to be harmed; even further, we are to invite ourselves to be harmed even though we don't deserve to be harmed. Turning the other cheek requires us to stand our ground, not run away, not hit back or ask someone else to fight for us. But why?

Our common sense says this is folly. Is it merely because we will go to heaven? No, we do not do this merely hoping for a heavenly reward; the reward will come, sooner or later, in this world. Injustice will be conquered. The better part of people's nature will be stirred to shame at their own unjust actions and laws, at their own intolerance and prejudice, and that stirring will transform their hearts and minds in a way that intellectual arguments never could. That stirring will transform their hearts and minds in a way that a violent response never could. Therefore, nonviolent protests which generate such shame are vital to the Movement, and are overlooked by others who pursue a more legalistic/legislative campaign, and obliterated by those who take to violence.

This means nonviolent protesters will sooner or later experience unearned suffering. It is a sacrifice on many levels, but one that must be made to redeem segregationists from their prejudice and cruelty, and ultimately to redeem society from systemic racism. By forcing someone acting unjustly and cruelly to witness undeserved suffering, nonviolent protest means to stir up that person's conscience (and from a more Christian perspective, to stir up the Holy Spirit within that person). When that happens, people feel a motivation, from within, to change.

The SCLC position sees itself as realistic in several ways. It is realistic in understanding the challenge of confronting and defeating segregation. But it also harbors a realistic hope that people can be redeemed, that America can become a more just country and a land of mutual respect and friendship. But it does not underestimate the cost of this goal to protesters. The sacrifice will be real and painful, and yet, it is one that faith calls for and one that, in the end, will bear the fruit of a beloved community.

Student Nonviolent Coordinating Committee (SNCC)

SNCC grew out the sit-in movement that was a more or less spontaneous expression of defiance of the injustice of segregation. Nevertheless, its position resembles some aspects of the SCLC position. Indeed, early statements of purpose regarding SNCC describe it as, in many ways, as a youth movement of nonviolent resistance to the evils of segregation. It may appear to be a student arm of SCLC for this reason. The aims and methods of some of the early members, especially those who had worked in the Nashville Sit-In Movement, were inspired by a position much like that of SCLC.

But SCLC did not orchestrate the sit-in movement, and the move to form SNCC came, in part, from an effort by Ella Baker, who had worked with SCLC, to encourage students to think and act independently of SCLC and other civil rights groups. Generally, SNCC members came from a different background than that of SCLC that shaped a different world view. They understood the nonviolent method and practiced it, but they generally did not have the kind of optimism that SCLC had with regard to redeeming the character of segregationists and reforming American society into a paradise of equality, mutual respect and friendship. They saw all too clearly what they faced in the response of segregationists to their nonviolent tactics.

While some SNCC leaders were more committed to the position of SCLC, over the years more and more grew less optimistic about the methods used. More and more saw nonviolence not so much as a means for redeeming others from a sinful character and way of life, but as an affirmation of one's own humanity in the face of cruelty and oppression. Nonviolence defies the authorities of an unjust system. It demonstrates that one is not afraid, and more, that one is better than such unjust authorities are.

This position is not so optimistic about American policy or even about the character of American people generally. It expresses much more frustration with the reality of American prejudice and racism than that of SCLC and certainly than that of the NAACP. Not many members of SNCC were part of the NAACP, but many SCLC members were also part of NAACP.

The SNCC position looked to actions that assumed, effused and radiated not merely a sense of equal respect and worth as human beings, but a sense of outshining the bully and oppressor and declaring that one's conduct is nobler. It includes a recognition that many Americans have racism so engrained in their character that "unearned suffering" may not be entirely effective, or effective at all, in stirring up the shame that Dr. King (and Gandhi) thought would be revealed. It was as if the character of such racists was drunk on its own prejudice and power, and in a drunken state, could not react with the shame Dr King thought would follow.

Dr. King and others might wait for that shame to kick in, but in the meantime, people are having their heads kicked in, people are being beaten and poked with electric cattle prods while locked up in jails. People are being taken at night to the middle of a field and shot dead. The crowds are not seeing that, and it is not part of a nonviolent protest *per se*. It is just violence, horrible violence. Like someone drunken and on a rampage, there is no reasoning with them (which SCLC already knew) but from this point of view, there is no shame stirred up in them.

What exists is the loss of African-American lives, fathers, mothers, siblings, who are hurt or killed and cannot provide for the family and the community because of that. Why allow that to happen? Why not defy the oppressors nonviolently, but hold their wild prejudice in check by letting them know you can and will defend yourself? They can 'respect' that, and perhaps that will sober them up enough to pay attention to your message better, sober them up enough to be ready to experience the redemptive shame that Dr. King and Gandhi advocate. You will still suffer, but you act in a way that is smart and doesn't allow the baser parts of their racist personalities to get the better of them. You show them who you are realistically, both sides: the nonviolent protester who may be able to shame them, but also the ordinary person with a right and responsibility to defend himself and those around him when threatened. Perhaps they can identify better with the latter, and sometime come around to understanding the former. Members of SNCC are still committed to not bearing arms; but many welcome the help of groups such as the Deacons of Defense and Justice who are armed and have successfully protected African-American communities from hate groups such as the KKK.

Even Dr. King applied for a gun license during the Montgomery Bus Boycott when he worried about the safety of his family. Gandhi may have insisted that nonviolence fill one's private life as well as one's public life, but Dr. King saw a need to protect his family. SNCC's position was to affirm that need, that right. It is only natural for a human being to protect his or her loved ones, and nonviolent protests must not be so construed as to convince people to turn away from a perfectly natural right.

Whether racists understood it or not, SNCC members were moved by a need to express their humanity in the large sense; not just by acting with nonviolence, but acting with nonviolence and then surviving to come home to a refrigerator that needs filled, a meal that needs cooked and children who need a bedtime story.

If you sacrifice so much of who you are as a person, others will not see you are a person. They already don't. Demonstrate equality and expect respect; SNCC members felt that having the means to protect themselves was a way to do that. It broke the mold of the African-American as a second-class citizen. The reality was that Africa-Americans were expected to act deferentially toward European-Americans, regardless of age or other status. Nonviolent protests were not, in themselves, deferential, but when they were coached to allow themselves to be pushed around, to being treated inhumanely, they resembled that deferential way of living, and SNCC members saw that as insulting and counterproductive.

SCLC's goal of the beloved community seemed, to SNCC members generally (perhaps not John Lewis and a few others) as too hard to swallow; too optimistic about what could be accomplished. Yes, nonviolence could shame people into changing unjust laws and practices, but it could not weave together a beloved community. If I am ashamed, I'm thinking of myself, my ways, etc. Those ways need to change, yes, but do I feel I need to make new friends? Why should I? My friendships weren't the problem; it was how I treated people of another race, another ethnicity. The SNCC faction believes that SCLC thinks nonviolent tension is a cure-all, but it only cures part of the problem. It can uncover injustice and help change unjust practices; but by itself, it does not make people friends; that's something more personal than a sense of shame can bring about. How many of your friendships were formed because you felt ashamed about yourself?

You can shame someone into recognizing and righting injustice, but you can't shame them into liking you and being a good friend to you. That's a more personal commitment. SNCC's position reflects this difference between SNCC and SCLC: agreeing on nonviolent tactics and changing unjust laws and customs, but disagreeing on how to establish a beloved community and on the role of nonviolence in one's life outside of life as a protester. In effect, I can protest nonviolently and put myself at risk. There will always be risk, and I accept that. But I can and should use my intelligence and other abilities to minimize that risk when possible, and certainly not become so passive in my actions that I, indirectly, encourage the emergence of greater risk for myself and others. If my behavior will be interpreted as a green light for even greater violence toward me, why behave like that? To be ready and able to fight back when attacked is still to be nonviolent first. It is still a sacrifice: someone else may throw the first punch or brick. I accept that risk. But if someone knows I won't throw the brick back, they may be emboldened to throw more, to do more violence than they would if they saw me as willing to protect myself at some point. If nonviolent protests are so choreographed as to, indirectly, encourage more boldness and violence, shame will never set in and African-American people, families and communities will suffer from the loss of life and resources that will follow. Why wait for a beloved community that will never truly happen, when we can build up African-American businesses and schools and communities starting right now?

Introduction to Module 1
Dorchester 1963: The Struggle for Nonviolent Tension and Opening Narrative

The success of Civil Rights campaigns in the 50s, such as the Montgomery Bus Boycott, inspired further activities in the 1960s. The student sit-ins to desegregate lunch counters in Greensboro, NC, in early 1960, were an example of a nonviolent protest that struck a chord, with both supporters and detractors. People who supported the students, often students themselves, saw it as a polite effort to do sometime fairly simple and fundamental: eat at a lunch counter. The students who openly broke the segregation laws were not demanding food for free; they asked politely and had money to pay, just as anyone might. It seemed absurd that such a basic need would be denied just because society was still in the habit of living out a system of segregation. Other students soon wanted to follow the example of those in the Greensboro Woolworth store.

But the sit-ins also drew the attention of local, European-Americans, some of whom decided to do their best to make the sit-in experience as unpleasant as possible, by harassing those who participated (whether the protesters were European-American or African-American). They poured ketchup and sugar on the protesters; some put out their cigarettes on the back of protester's necks. These were the less violent ones. Those people who were more violent used bats to harm some of the protesters.

Here, however, the protesters were drawing out the contradiction of the Jim Crow South. How could people claim that segregation was the best and most proper way to order relations in society, when it allowed such ignorance, hatred and violence to fester under a facade of civility? How could segregation be regarded as necessary to guard the moral purity of European-American children, if many of them could carry out such atrocious actions as they entered adulthood?

Drawing out this contradiction was difficult and dangerous, however. The emotional and physical toll on the protests themselves was high enough. But there was also the toll of going to jail, where the temperament of the police officers, in many cases, did not differ significantly from that of the local, European-Americans who had harassed them at the lunch counter.

Initially, organizers raised funds to make bail, but by early 1961, such efforts were draining money that civil rights organizations needed. Members of the Congress of Racial Equality (CORE) decided to reverse things and opt for "jail, not bail" in order to shift the financial strain away from civil rights organizations, and put it on the local, segregationist establishment instead. Tom Gaither, a CORE field secretary, led a group of students from Friendship Junior College in Rock Hill, SC, in a sit-in at a local McCrory's store. The majority did not post bail and spent a month on a prison farm doing menial labor, but their actions drew support, while taxing the resources of the establishment. They sang protest songs to keep their spirits up.

Some of this approach was used in the protests in Albany, GA, the following year. Albany, Georgia, was a city that had experienced a growth in its African-American population in recent years. In the 1930s, they had set up a chapter of the National Association for the Advancement of Colored People (NAACP) and had begun to work on voter registration, in an effort to secure some political power. Complaints had been raised about poor streets and sewer systems in the Lincoln Heights section of town, and about the segregated polling places, but without much success. A boycott of a local newspaper whose segregationist editor had offended the African-American community in an editorial had also been unsuccessful. Between 1961 and 1962, however, the Southern Christian Leadership Conference (SCLC) and the Student Nonviolent Coordinating Committee (SNCC) organized protest activities to address an array of problems and ultimately to end segregation.

One of the initial problems was, in some ways, generational. African-American adults in Albany who had leadership positions in local the chapter of the NAACP and similar organizations did not collaborate well with the younger SNCC organizers who had come to town. Some felt that their community already had organizations in place, and were doing their best to address problems themselves. Some distrusted outsiders who were unaware of the local history. Two SNCC organizers, Charles Sherrod and Cordell Reagon, began to devote less time to working with adults in Albany, and more time trying to organize high school and college-age members of the African-American community. This seemed to further distance them from adults in the community, some of whom did not want to be seen with the SNCC organizers in public. Officials at the local Albany State College tried to discourage students from working with SNCC, eventually dismissing some and threatening to expel others. The adults in the African-American community, by and large, also seemed uncomfortable with the kinds of activities that SNCC was planning, such as testing local compliance with the new Interstate Commerce Commission's regulations banning segregation at places of interstate travel (regulations prompted by the bloody "freedom rides" that CORE, SCLC and SNCC had carried out recently).

Led by the NAACP chapter, local organizations in the African-American community joined forces to form The Albany Movement. Some attempt was made to smooth over relations with the SNCC people, but without much success. The NAACP wanted to use the legal methods it was more familiar with to work against the refusal of Albany officials to comply with the new ICC regulations against segregation. Three young people from the non-SNCC, Youth Council, volunteered to test the practice of segregation at the local bus station. Once arrested, their bail was paid by members of the Albany Movement and they were convicted in their local trial. Local NAACP officials appealed to the national organization for additional funds, but the national officials were not willing to give funds beyond those for the three volunteers to an organization that was not controlled by the local NAACP. They did not think that the Albany Movement would be as effective as the NAACP, and they were less than happy about SNCC involvement and activities in the area.

SNCC eventually initiated its own "freedom ride" to protest the segregated facilities at the local train station. They were met not only by police, but by a large crowd of local African-Americans. After several Freedom Riders were arrested and refused to post bail, more local people in the African-American community began to protest, especially younger people. As these protests grew, leaders in the Albany Movement contacted SCLC and asked for Dr. King to come to Albany and aid their cause. SNCC people who had spent a great deal of time and effort working locally were not enthused about bringing in what they considered outside help, but other local leaders argued that the protests needed funds that the local community could not afford, and that the help of an outside organization such as SCLC was necessary.

The effort to have speeches and marches that would result in filling up jails was, in some ways, thwarted by the way police reacted as much as by the non-cooperation of civil rights groups. Police Chief Pritchett was able to keep the Ku Klux Klan from intervening in a destructive manner, and he had ordered his officers to avoid verbal and physical abuse when they arrested protesters. He also had them jailed in a variety of places outside Albany, so that local jails were not filled beyond capacity. Dr. Martin Luther King Jr., who initially had only planned a short stay, was jailed several times, but when he refused to pay his bail, it was eventually paid by someone from the establishment. They clearly did not want Dr. King in their jails. Since protesters were treated nonviolently, federal officials had not become involved. Also, when there were negotiations, African-American leaders, including King, failed to get an agreement in writing. When protests were eventually called off, the town establishment's version of the agreement differed significantly from that of the movement's leaders. With nothing stated and signed in writing, little change was achieved, other than the release of about 700 protesters from jail.

In the wake of what some regard as a failure and a slowing down in the momentum of the civil rights movement, King and others decided that they needed to meet face to face to discuss what would be the best way to go forward. A retreat at Dorchester, GA, was planned for 1963, so that SCLC and others could better plan how to move forward with protests in Birmingham, AL, Louisville, KY, or wherever.

For the purpose of our game, the Dorchester 1963 module assumes more diversity in the civil rights groups that attended Dorchester than was the case historically, in order to represent more of the ideas and methods which were being discussed in the larger Civil Rights community, at the time.

Opening Narrative: Dorchester 1963

There are rocks on the roadside. Though you try to avoid them, one foot or the other keeps turning on a rock or a dusty bottle. The sun's almost down and you're lost in the outskirts of Savannah Georgia. As the cars pass by you try not to look, but somewhere in your heart, you know what's likely to happen next. Someone is going to stop, or call out. Some group of young white men out for a wild time will discover you, a black man walking alone on the roadside, and their fun will begin.

Why do you get involved! You could have stayed at home in North Carolina, doing your little part in the Civil Rights Struggle, but doing it where people know you, and where you always know where to go when there's danger. You're not afraid of confrontation. You were one of the students who took part in the Lunch-counter sit-ins in Greensboro. You refused to leave your seats in the white-only section after you'd been told you'd get nothing. You put up with the local boys' insults, the punches, the ketchup and sugar poured on you, and you held your ground. You were looking beyond their anger, beyond your own anger, because you had a fiery ideal that nonviolent tension could change the hearts of people as misguided and mean as any of these kids. If things got worse, you knew you were on home ground; you were fighting, nonviolently, on familiar turf, and that made a difference. Even now, walking on the side of Georgia road, you still could feel the warm pride of the work you'd done back home.

But now you were in Georgia. You'd been here once to visit relatives, but that was long ago, and under different circumstances. You were not on friendly ground, and you could feel it. An unwritten rule in the South said that a black man should not be out at night near white neighborhoods; the local boys kept their eyes open for such opportunities. Each time a car passed, you imagined a beer bottle crashing into the back of your head, or a car unloading, figures approaching. There; the sun's down and the twilight has settled in.

Suddenly, headlights swerve behind you. A car stops and one door opens. Maybe it's not a crowd of white boys; maybe just the police. But then again, is that any better? You're not from this town, you're not from this state, and no one knows where you are to come looking for you. You keep walking, until…

"Hey, hey there son."

You keep walking.

"Hey, now is that you Freddy? Freddy Walker?"

Your name! You turned around, now placing the voice with a memory of meeting a Greensboro Sunday School teacher with huge hands, a huge heart and a bellowing voice. "Jim..Jim Williams, is that you?

"Fred; how come you let your car break down like that; that's just not a good excuse 'round here."

"Oh I know it; I know it."

The two of you get in Jim's car and start driving.

"You're heading for Dorchester aren't ya"

"Well, that's what I started out to do, but…"

"Hey, I got a cousin fifteen minutes from here; we'll get that car running and then you're off."

"Well I appreciate your help Jim, but…I don't know. I'm getting a bad feeling about this. This is too far from home, you know what I mean?

"Keep talkin'; keep talkin'"

"Oh, I should just go to sleep I guess…"

"Yeah, yeah that's what some of them white folks like to hear; black folks snoring instead of protesting!"

You laugh, and, looking at Jim's big knuckles gripping the wheel, realize that you weren't the only one who set out alone for the retreat at Dorchester. After the lukewarm results of the Albany Campaign, the leaders of the Southern Christian Leadership Conference decided that before they took their protests to Birmingham Alabama, also know as Bomb-ingham, or Louisville, KY, or anywhere else, they would meet at Dorchester to review strategies, and plan on how to generate more of a success. The big names would be there later on, but you were going early as a staffer to help plan out what would be discussed among the various groups who each had a different opinion of how the civil rights movements should move forward.

You feel you have to break the silence. "I mean, It's one thing to be taking it to the establishment in Greensboro; that's close; it's home ground. But Birmingham…"

"You'd rather get the hell beat out of you in Greensboro than in Birmingham?"

You both laugh. "Well now let's not talk about that 'till the sun comes up, okay."

Jim smiles. "Okay. But that's a good point; a man's gonna die fighting for justice, it just feels better to do the dying at home, don't it?

"Yeah, but you know what I'm saying Jim. This stuff we're doing; it's hard; it's hard. I can't believe I do these protests without punching out some of the idiots who follow us around."

"Keep talking, keep talkin'."

"I mean…ahh. It was all I could do to keep it together back home, but here. And then in Birmingham! It's not gonna happen; I just know it's not gonna happen. I see one more a'them toothy, grinning—"

"Okay, okay. You know why we're down here."

"I know why someone's got to come down here; I don't know why it's me and you that's got to come down here. I can do it back home, but here it just feels like I'm gonna be someone's kicking post. Just some block of wood getting kicked around like I'm nothing, and I'm just gonna sit there and take it? I mean I know all the reasons Dr. King and others have, and I think he's right most of the time."

"But not this time?"

You stare at the darkness out the window; the stars are emerging above the trees. Jim answers for you.

"Maybe, huh. And that's the real reason you came, isn't it? Not to protest and boycott, but to find out what you should do, what we all should do, and find someone to tell you it's worth it so it sticks. Isn't that it?

You don't even have to answer him; he said it better than you had said it to yourself a hundred times on this drive. You're going to Dorchester with a doubt in your heart and a lump in your throat. But now you've got company, and your curious again, about what you find when you reach Dorchester. As Jim starts humming one of the freedom songs, you close your eyes and sleep.

Introduction to Module 2
Memphis 1966: The Struggle for Black Power
and Opening Narrative

The Civil Rights struggle had some notable high points-the Supreme Court's *Brown v Board of Education* decision in 1954, engineered by the NAACP;[1] the Montgomery, Alabama Bus Boycott of 1957, out of which Dr. Martin Luther King, Jr.'s SCLC[2] was born; the student sit-ins of the 1960s, out of which SNCC[3] was born; and the March on Washington of 1963, in which all three organizations cooperated.

But other advances were purchased with tragedy.

The Freedom Rides of the early 1960s saw civil rights activists and students shockingly brutalized by local racist whites, with the complicity of local and sometimes federal law enforcement. The lack of protection afforded by the federal government, and particularly the FBI[4], left a lasting impression on the movement's most militant activists, including Howard University student Stokeley Carmichael and CORE[5] leader James Farmer, who participated in the Freedom Rides and was jailed in Parchman, Mississippi's maximum security prison as a consequence.

President John F. Kennedy's administration took steps in 1961 and 1962 to ensure minority rights in voting, employment, housing, transportation, and education by executive order. The stage was set for a new legislative initiative to deal with the problem of federal protection of civil rights. After President Kennedy was assassinated, President Johnson became a strong supporter of civil rights and pushed several landmark bills through Congress. The most important of these are the Civil Rights Act of 1964, the Voting Rights Act of 1965, and the Fair Housing Act of 1968.

The Civil Rights Act of 1964 was in many ways a memorial to assassinated President John F. Kennedy, who himself had been moved to propose the legislation in 1963. In the spring of 1963, President Kennedy was sickened and embarrassed by nationally televised images of peaceful demonstrators in Birmingham, Alabama being beaten, attacked by police dogs, sprayed with water hoses, then arrested and jailed.[6]

---

[1] The National Association for the Advancement of Colored People, founded 1909, was based in the black middle class and on the participle of leadership by the community's "talented tenth." In the rural South, NAACP leaders were typically Pullman porters, teachers, and owners of small business.

[2] The Southern Christian Leadership Conference, founded 1957, was an organization of Southern black preachers, predominantly Baptist.

[3] The Student Nonviolent Coordinating Committee was founded in 1961, a loose network of students from Historically Black Colleges and Universities (HBCUs). Their focus in the rural South was the unorganized population, primarily tenant farmers and sharecroppers, the elderly and high school students, as most able-bodied young men had left looking for work in cities of the North and South.

[4] FBI Director J. Edgar Hoover, in turn, was convinced that the entire civil rights movement was a Communist plot, and adhered to that belief until his death in 1972.

[5] The Congress of Racial Equality (Founded 1942) by a group of pacifists and labor organizers.

Concerned about the country's international reputation during the Cold War, Kennedy sent a major piece of civil rights legislation to Congress on June 19, 1963. The bill faced fierce opposition in both the House and Senate.

The March on Washington took place in August, 1963, and President Kennedy was assassinated in November. The Civil Rights Act, signed into law by President Johnson July 2nd, 1964, was viewed by some as a tribute to the slain President. The Civil Rights Act of 1964 addressed discrimination, chiefly in public accommodations and employment.

Importantly, the Civil Rights Act of 1964 was principally based not on the Fourteenth Amendment, but rather on the Commerce clause. As such, the "state action" limitations of the Fourteenth Amendment (per the Court's ruling in the *Civil Rights Cases*) do not apply, and the actions of private citizens are thus covered. It does mean, however, that the activities regulated must affect, or have some effect upon intestate commerce. This effect was buttressed by making the Act applicable to any person, program or entity that received federal funds (Title VI). Some of the more important provisions of the 1964 Civil Rights Act include Titles II, VI, and VII. Title II makes it illegal for the provider of any public accommodation (restaurants, hotels, public transportation) to discriminate against a potential customer or client on the basis of race. The government agency with primary jurisdiction over Title II is the Civil Rights Division of the U.S. Department of Justice. Title VI of the 1964 Act (Nondiscrimination in Federally-Assisted or Sponsored Programs) makes it illegal for the provider or sponsor of any federally assisted program (including hospitals) to discriminate against a potential customer or client on the basis of race. The government agency with primary jurisdiction over Title VI is the Civil Rights Division of the U.S. Department of Justice. Title VII of the 1964 Act states prevents an employer from discriminating against any person because of race, color, religion, sex, or national origin. This applies to hiring, firing, promotions, pay, training, or other workplace conditions. The government agency with primary jurisdiction over Title VII is the Equal Employment Opportunity Commission (EEOC).

While legislation was being advanced, registration was advancing as well, but at a high cost. The Mississippi Freedom Summer of 1964, while registering large numbers of black people who had never before voted, opened with the brutal murder of three civil rights workers by a mob in Philadelphia, MS., in which the Sheriff, Cecil Price, was actively involved.[7]

After this kind of sacrifice, participants in the summer voter registration drive were sharply disappointed at the 1964 Democratic Convention when their bid to seat an integrated "Freedom" delegation in place of Mississippi's segregated one was rebuffed. It was clear to them that candidate Lyndon Johnson was behind this, seeking to keep Southern voters from bolting the Party. His running mate Hubert Humphrey brought them offers of a compromise-seating two "at large" delegates and explicit instructions that outspoken local activist Fannie Lou Hamer be not

---

[6] The Birmingham demonstrations marked a new, high-profile strategy by SCLC to focus the attention of the nation on Southern segregation through confrontations in which nonviolent demonstrators met the most violent perpetrators of segregation head-on. The Birmingham disturbances were broadcast on nationwide TV, and were seen all over the world, creating a public relations disaster for America, which sought to lead the Free World.

[7] Freedom Summer was sponsored by the "Conference of Federated Organizations ("COFO") a temporary alliance of the NAACP, SCLC, CORE and SNCC.

admitted. Rejecting the compromise, it became hard for many members of SNCC to trust white politicians at all after this.

The 1965 Voting Rights Act passed in the wake of the Los Angeles Riots, which left 50 square blocks of the city leveled as if it had been bombed. The 1968 Fair Housing Act passed in the wake of the riots that erupted after the assassination of Dr. Martin Luther King, Jr.

The Movement since then has been hard pressed to find moments uniquely suited to celebration. There are reasons for this, rooted in the historical context of the time as well as in the strategic and tactical decisions made by movement leadership. We will use as an example the response of the civil rights leadership to James Meredith's decision to show that blacks no longer needed be afraid in Mississippi, by embarking on a "March Against Fear," from Memphis, Tennessee, to Jackson, Mississippi, a distance of over two hundred miles.

Meredith was still hated in Mississippi as the first black to integrate Ole Miss, under heavy federal guard. On the second day of his march, only a few miles into the Mississippi border, a white racist pumped four rounds of bird shot into Meredith with a shotgun, yelling "I only want James Meredith" as reporters and members of Meredith's entourage dived for cover. Meredith was hospitalized in Memphis, in serious, but not critical condition.

Word of the shooting reached participants at a White House Conference, "To Fulfill These Rights." The conference had been convened by President Lyndon Johnson after a 1965 speech to the graduating class of Howard University, in which he promised to move the cause of civil rights forward in a massive way. Several of the leaders present at the conference, including Roy Wilkins of the NAACP and Dr. Martin Luther King, Jr. of SCLC, flew to Memphis to consult with Meredith, and there decided to continue his March. Floyd McKissick, the new Chair of CORE, had already pledged to do so, and a call went out to Stokeley Carmichael, newly elected Chairmen of SNCC, for his organization to participate as well.

All the leaders met at the Lorraine Motel in Memphis, the site at which MLK was shot to death only two years later, to discuss strategy. Wilkins, King, and Carmichael were the key players in the discussions, and the simulation focuses on their meetings.

Each participant has role instructions regarding the personal background, preferred issues, and organizational imperatives that affected each leader. The participants are not required to make the same choices as the historical character, but they must be true to the character. The idea is to discuss and reflect upon the issues, and make a principled choice based on what we know of history, these leaders, and what has happened since.

Opening Narrative: Memphis 1966

The scenery passes by easily; the bus slips through the countryside like smoke through a screen. As your thoughts begin to settle, your attention withdraws to the bus windows themselves, and you see that one is broken. How did that happen? You know that it could have been anything; a stone from a truck up ahead, the jolt from a pothole below. Anything. But this bus is special; it's the first bus you've taken on a long trip since you took part in a freedom ride, and as you gaze on that broken window, you recall the shock and disgust you'd felt, and the fear. That was some years ago, and you consider the bus itself again. Could it be one of the ones that protected freedom riders like yourself from the vicious hailstorm of hatred that had rained just outside? No crowds will be waiting for you when this bus stops. You won't have to wait to use the ladies' room until a group of you all had to go. You won't worry about the slashed tires blowing out somewhere in the countryside, with a line of cars waiting for the bus to pull over. This trip is so normal that it feels strange.

But your destination is anything but normal. You are going to Memphis, Tennessee, not for the music or the food primarily, but for James Meredith. In 1962, after the efforts of Governor Ross Barnett to stop him had clashed with the efforts of President Kennedy to protect and help him, Meredith became the first African-American (also Native-American) to attend and graduate from the University of Mississippi. More recently, in 1966, he planned a March Against Fear walk from Memphis, Tennessee to Jackson Mississippi. He was not acting with Civil Rights Organizations, but when he was shot on the first day of his walk, a number of Civil Rights Organizations decided to reach out to him (he did not die, but was hurt) and perhaps continue the March that he began.

You are part of the advance team that is meeting in Memphis to see if there is enough agreement among people to carry out a large, coordinated March. But while there is some agreement that the march should go on; you know there will be disagreement about its purpose, and the means used to carry it forward. You realize that a woman seated just in front of that broken window has glanced at you, probably more than once, and you've been staring.

"I'm sorry." you say quickly, anticipating an awkward situation. She nods, then looks at you, squinting her eyes a little.

"Diane? Is that you Diane Williams?"

Suddenly, she looks familiar. "Oh my word; Ella?"

The seat beside her is empty, and almost forgetting to grab your purse, you move across the aisle and give her a hug before sitting down.

"Oh my, Diane…just a few years and we're already getting old and forgetting people we should know."

"I know, I know; oh, now tell me how you've been since Nashville." You knew that Ella had worked with SNCC further South after the Nashville sit-ins that you'd both participated in, but she fills in a few details you didn't know about, while you let her know what had been going on in Nashville since she left. You and Ella had never been the closest of friends in Nashville, but you were friendly. Both of you had been at Dorchester, roughly three years ago, and after a few miles roll by, Ella starts to chuckle.

"I was sitting here, and I just, kind of, felt this heat on the side of my face--"
"—What?"
"—And I looked over and saw this woman staring at me—"
"Now, you know I didn't mean to stare at--"
"and I thought, 'this woman's gonna try to steal my earrings!'"

"Oh heavens!"

"—the way you were staring." She smiles, and then you laugh as you glance back at the window.

"They are nice earrings?" you say.

"Well, I know these bus trips can put me right to sleep sometimes." she suggests.

"Yes, well….It's funny Ella." You shift around in your seat, and Ella quietly waits for you to continue. "I was just looking at that broken window up there."

"What? Oh yeah, look at that."

"It just…well, brought up memories of that ride I took."

Ella tilts her head from left to right and leans closer. "Diane, you mean one of the freedom rides?"

"This is…this is my first bus ride of any length since then."

"Oh no?"

"I saw that broken win--" your voice breaks a little, and you feel Ella's warm hand on your shoulder, as a wave of feelings rushes across your face. But it's only for a moment; you're okay.

Ella tries to get you talking: "Now, I've forgotten when you took that ride."

You close your eyes for a second as you answer her: "I was at Anniston."

"Oh no."

"Not the first bus, thank goodness, though we didn't fare a great deal better. You know, I was just staring at that window and thinking how such a little thing can bring back so many memories."

Now Ella was squinting at you again. "So, you took a car to Dorchester…"

"Um-hum."

"…and now, you're on this bus."

"Yes."

"Diane, I'm almost sure we're going the same way today."

"Isn't that how a bus works?"

"No, no; I mean you're going to Memphis for the meeting about Meredith's March."

You look at her and shake you're head. "You too?" You both chuckle.

"Yes, well," she explains with some bravado, "you know, someone's got to set up the coffee pots!"

"Oh really!"

"Yes, yes, and the sugar--, oh my, someone's got to get the sugar on the table for everyone."

"Ella, you--" as you make your comment, a white man with grayish-white hair, reddish cheeks and glasses turns around in his seat, a few rows up, and stares at you until you both look down. After a little while he shakes his head and turns back around abruptly. You both feel the need to keep the conversation going, but more discreetly, in lower voices.

"There are still lots of folks," Ella whispers, "who just can't stomach coffee integrated with sugar!"

"Um-hum." you chuckle quietly as you squeeze your lips together thinking about that man a few rows up.

"Those men keeping you busy in SNCC, Ella?"

"You know, some things never change. Rights for the black man now--"

"Oh yes."

"—yesterday,"

51

"I hear ya."

"But the black woman…is still better at making coffee, so…"

"I know; time will come though. Is that Carmichael who is the chairperson now?" you ask.

"Yes he is. SNCC is a good group. A few of them are talking a lot of militancy these days. A lot of them just want to build up their communities; show we can take the high road compared to the folks who want to keep us down. Most of the Nashville people who were there from the beginning are long gone. I'm sure Lawson's more than a little concerned. That man is so committed to the nonviolence you know.

"I know, I know." she agrees. "But I am glad to see new people getting involved! Ella, it's just that everyone, each group, seems to have good projects, but there is so much movement in different directions."

"And that's bad?"

"Well, no; it doesn't have to be bad." You reply. "The Lord works in mysterious ways--"

"Oh yes."

"Each one's got to do what they do best; bear their cross…." You pause. "But you know, there's so much going on now; Dr. King coming out against the War; folks losing patience with the pace of things; even folks losing patience with the impatient ones….My, oh my….But, you know, we've got CORE people like myself, SNCC, SCLC and the NAACP, and a few others, all coming together to try to carry on this March, but how are we going to be united with so many different views and commitments?"

You both pause. Then, you hear Ella begin to sing, very quietly, "Ain't Gonna Let Nobody Turn Me 'Round," but with the words changed to "Ain't gonna let no infighting, lordy, turn me 'round." You smile, and very quietly join in.

When you finish, Ella leans closer, "I don't think I've ever heard a freedom song sung so quietly!"

"Well we're in a bus, not a jail." You reply.

Ella adds, with a wink, "…for now."

The bus keeps rolling on its way, of course, but you have a smile on your lips more often than not. You feel more confident that folks will find a way to work together to carry on Meredith's March. You glance out the windows, watching the shadow of the bus slide through the countryside like smoke through a screen.

Appendix I:
Civil Rights History and
the Long Road Already Traveled

(Dr. June Finer and others, Selma to Montgomery March, 1965, © 1976 Matt Herron/Take Stock / The Image Works)

Subchapters:
a. Early Slavery Laws and Practices
b. Resistance to Slavery
c. Dred Scott (1856)
d. Civil Rights Act of 1875 and Reconstruction
e. End of Reconstruction and Compromise of 1877
f. Plessy v. Ferguson (1896)
g. Segregation (Jim Crow Laws)
h. Wartime segregation
i. Brown v. Board of Education (1954)

Early Slavery Laws and Practices

Slavery, in a variety of forms, can be traced through history to many different places and populations, but in relation to the Civil Rights Movement, we can begin by understanding slavery in Colonial America. The practice of keeping slaves and indentured servants is recorded as early as 1619 in Jamestown, Virginia. When European countries were setting up colonies on the East coast of America, slaves and indentured servants included Africans, Native Americans, as well as white Europeans who had been in prison. But it soon became obvious that the latter two groups would not be a reliable source of cheap labor. Native Americans knew the land, of course, and could escape fairly easily. Taking them as slaves also stirred up the anger of nearby tribes, putting some settlements in danger of retaliation. Furthermore, the animosity created by such slavery hurt the fur trade with Native people, which Europeans coveted. While white slaves and indentured servants were more accustomed to the work they would have to do, had much stronger immunities to European diseases, and were more familiar with the ways of the culture, they also blended in with other white Europeans, so again, escape was fairly easy compared to escape for Africans forced into slavery. Keeping Europeans, as slaves, who had friends and family in Europe could cause trouble back home, as well. Furthermore, both groups, Native Americans and white Europeans, were small in number compared to the need for laborers.

Africans forced into slavery, on the other hand, could be taken far from their homelands, to places unfamiliar to them, and far from friends and family. Their physical appearance and language made it extremely unlikely that they could blend in with other colonists, and unlikely they could get word back home to warn others of the practice. The number of Africans who could, theoretically, be captured and enslaved was much greater than the number of Native Americans or white Europeans. European greed and guns empowered some African tribes to capture members of rival tribes and sell them into slavery. Vincent Harding describes how European schemes to draw "Black Gold" out of Africa created power imbalances, deceit and destruction. Given these factors, Africans became the slave of choice, and they soon began to replace white European slaves and indentured servants.

Nevertheless, it was not easy to 'convince' Africans to agree to their enslaved condition. White society took conscious steps to transform free people into slaves, and develop a 'slave mentality' in them. Among other things, they sought to ingrain a sense of African inferiority and white European superiority into the enslaved Africans, and their children. They also wanted African slaves to feel impotent and dependent on their "owners," to the point of putting the owner's welfare on par with their own. This effort 'worked' in the sense that it became a kind of social conditioning and brainwashing that enslaved people had to struggle to rise above.

What kind of people, and what kind of mentality, could be the catalyst for such inhumane action and sentiment? Part of it was, of course, greed. The profits from colonizing the New World, including those from agriculture, especially tobacco, the mining of precious metals, etc., were even more lucrative when the labor to do so was, from one point of view, free.

At the same time, there was also a sense of mission and of superiority that white Europeans had with regard to anyone not European. The brutality of slavery paralleled the brutality of Native American relations. Native tribes who had helped white Europeans when they'd first arrived on the continent, were later brutally destroyed. Furthermore, physical strength and technology (and the maddening conviction to use them in such ways) were not the only means used by white Europeans.

Some white Europeans, no doubt, were herded to the New World by others, and when they found themselves struggling to survive, they became afraid and reacted with violence. But others, no doubt, knew that this would be the case. Nevertheless, instead of finding ways to live with each other in Europe, people with religious and political differences, as well people looking for economic gain, came to the New World for a kind of peace, even if it meant stealing the land from Native Americans and enslaving Africans to settle it and exploit its riches. Physical, psychological, and legal means, all means necessary, were used in this effort.

While slavery would eventually be limited to Africans, the change in legal status did not happen immediately. Initially, in the early 1600s, Africans in America could be found in a broad spectrum of social status: from slaves to indentured servants to free men and women. That spectrum was narrowed down as white Europeans committed to using Africans as cheap labor for raising cash crops, among other things. A series of laws in the 1630s, first in Virginia and then elsewhere, limited African rights and status until the only status left was that of lifelong slavery. There were laws forbidding interracial marriage, laws against Africans owning property, especially weapons, laws against the right of Africans to assemble, as well as laws declaring that slavery of African parents would also be conferred on their children. Furthermore, as part of the "social conditioning" mentioned above, there were laws against African religious practices, language, dancing and the use of drums; as well as laws against Africans defending themselves in any way from the violence of white Europeans against them. In addition, laws were passed to make it clear that conversion to Christianity would have no affect on slave status. These laws set Africans apart from white Europeans in their behavior as well as in their livelihood, and they also gave lower-class white Europeans a false sense of solidarity with the upper-class white Europeans who were benefiting the most from the whole social arrangement.

Resistance to Slavery

From the very beginning, Africans resisted slavery in every way possible. Slave ships close to the African shore experienced uprisings, with Africans using anything, including their own chains, as weapons. Out in the ocean, there were more uprisings. Sometimes African women, who were often kept on deck by the white crew for less than noble purposes, acted as lookouts to help time the attack for the best chance of success. Success was not easy, especially since the crew had access to guns and other weapons, and those who attempted a revolt and were stopped were often killed in brutal ways, in front of other Africans on board. There are reports of some successful revolts in which Africans were able to take command and return to Africa, but not many.

For some, resistance took the form of suicide. Some, after unsuccessful attempts to get free, retreated deep into the ship cargo holds and refused food until death. There are records of Africans who leaped into the sea, joyful that they had at least escaped, despite the fact that they were surrounded by ocean with no hope of swimming to any land. Sharks often followed slave ships, so that the dancing jubilation of Africans who escaped into the water was short-lived. Indeed, in their concern for not losing so much 'cargo,' the white European crew watched the Africans carefully for signs of jumping, and they devised nets to try to prevent jumpers from making it off the ship. Some of the white Europeans who witnessed the revolts and suicides could not understand the reason, unless it was due to the strain and boredom of the journey. Most did not understand the idea that Africans, like any other people, cherished freedom.

Indeed, this yearning for freedom became all the more ironic during the Revolutionary period in American history. As the idea of self-rule and democracy spread among English colonists in the 18th century, and revolution become more and more on people's minds, Africans living as slave also heard the call and felt some hope. The equality of men, the right of people to govern themselves; these ideals could be applied to any human being, not just white Europeans. During the Revolutionary War, especially in the North, there were petitions, speeches and court cases by black people, pointing out the incongruity of democratic rhetoric and slavery. The "social conditioning" that had been imposed on so many Africans, had not changed their natural awareness of their own mental and physical abilities, nor had it habituated all to conformity and silence. Some saw their equality in their understanding of Christian Scripture, and when it was rejected by white Christians, they formed their own churches. Even some white Europeans made the connection and declared, in 1774 at the First Continental Congress, that the country would discontinue and wholly separate its commerce from the Slave Trade. But once the war was over, the newly independent white Americans enacted the Constitution in 1787, which not only protected the institution of slavery by guaranteeing the right of slave-owners to track down escaped slaves across state lines, and by promising federal troops to put down insurrections, but also made a fraction of the number of slaves (three-fifths) a part of how Congressional representation would be determined. The clash between democratic ideals and the institution of slavery, as well as the service of blacks in the Revolutionary Army, was overlooked as the leaders of the new country realized the economic and political advantages of allowing slavery to continue.

Some people found ways to take the matter into their own hands by escaping, and for a long time Florida was a haven for those being oppressed by the white Americans. Native Americans, as well as black Americans, not only avoided white American authority, but used the territory as a base of operation for raids and attacks on the Southern states. Eventually, beginning in 1816, American gunboats and troops denied native and black Americans their safe haven, reaching into what was then Spanish territory to reinforce continued domination over both populations.

Those escaping to the North believed that they would be much better off, and indeed, by 1830 slavery had been abolished in the North. But changing laws did not change prejudices and fears, and both continued to exist in the North. Former slaves who escaped North represented a source of labor that could compete for jobs that poorer, white Americans counted on. That economic pressure, as well as simple and strong racial prejudice, combined to put black Americans in the North in a precarious position. While they were "free," their rights were neither well defined, nor well protected. Many were not allowed on public lands; black children were denied access to public schools. Many black Americans were even denied the right to vote. Slave catchers from the South were often able to work within the laws to recapture and return those who had escaped; some even managed to take black Americans who had never been slaves in the first place.

At the community level, some black communities were denigrated by white community leaders as morally suspect and inferior. Mobs of white Americans sometimes acted to intimidate or physically force black Americans out of their communities. In addition, white organizations, such as the American Colonization Society encouraged black Americans to show appreciation for their African heritage by immigrating back to Africa. Indeed, these attempts to send black Americans to Africa led many to prefer terms other than "African-American" to refer to themselves, since they were determined to stay and thrive in the country that so many of their parents, grandparents and other ancestors had built with lifetimes of servitude, poverty and brutality.

In response, black Americans in the North acted in concert to protect each other, as well as aid those who had recently escaped from slavery in the South. In places such as Detroit, near the relative safety of Canada, and Philadelphia, which had a strong black community, people went out of their way to help fugitive slaves. Their actions conflicted with fugitive slave laws that required compliance with the return of escaped slaves. But many were willing to defy such laws and accept whatever punishment, rather than allow an escaped slave to be returned to servitude. So, while the institution of slavery did not exist in the North after 1830, laws, violence and prejudices existed in its place and created conditions which were economically, physically and psychologically arduous for black Americans in the North.

Among white Americans, in the North and South, there were abolitionists whose religious and moral beliefs fueled their activities to not only help escaped slaves, but attempt to abolish slavery altogether. There were manumission societies, in the upper South for the most part, as early as 1815. According to Benjamin Lundy, editor of a publication dedicated to universal emancipation, there were 106 emancipation societies in the slave states, but only 24 in the free states. Indeed, some people in the South felt that slavery was a kind of original sin that had been passed down from earlier generations; a feature of the cultural landscape that was unavoidable, ugly, but also cemented in the economy and overall way of life. The colonization societies, mentioned above, which sought to colonize freed slaves in West Africa (in what eventually became the country of Liberia) responded to the desire to move away from the institution of slavery. But it also appealed to those who supported slavery, as a way of removing "problem" slaves, while keeping the rest. The prospect of being "returned" to Africa was also, as mentioned above, very unpopular with black Americans who regarded the land of their birth, and of their parents' births, as their native land. In the North, some black Americans who had escaped slavery, such as Frederick Douglass, argued forcefully against slavery anywhere. White abolitionists, such as William Lloyd Garrison, set up Anti-Slavery Societies in New England and New York, and eventually the American Anti-Slavery Society. While the members of these societies worked in a pro-active manner to instigate debates about the institution of slavery, there were met, at times, by angry and violent crowds who either disliked black Americans or considered slavery a necessary evil for the economic reasons. The movement also struggled under internal disputes regarding issues that paralleled the abolition of slavery. For instance, in 1840, while Garrison and others argued that other reform movements (such as women's rights and temperance) needed to be linked to abolition, abolitionists from New York argued against them, some suggesting it was impractical to spread the movement's resources in so many directions, and others simply arguing against the equal participation of women in the Society's activities, in principle. Some abolitionist, despite their rhetoric, also treated black Americans within the organizations in a paternalistic manner.

National politics also played a role in the resistance to slavery, and the defense of slavery. By 1820, the number of free and slave states was equal, and a conscious effort was made to keep it that way. Positions on other issues would change, but as long as there was equality, especially in the Senate, with regard to slavery, the issue could be kept under wraps. This was the spirit of the Missouri Compromise of 1820, by which politicians agreed to boundaries on which states and territories of the country would be considered free or slave. And yet, some statesmen saw through these efforts to 'put off' the problem of slavery. Thomas Jefferson, toward the end of his life, told one friend that these compromise efforts were, to him, "like a firebell in the night" which heralded the end of the union itself. Indeed, other compromise efforts in Congress included the so-called "Gag Rule" in the House of Representatives, which (from 1836 to 1844) prevented serious discussion about abolishing slavery in the District of Columbia.

Westward expansion, however, seemed to be regarded as a birthright of the nation. The promise of agricultural and mineral resources, such as gold, furs, grain, lumber, cotton, cowhides and tallow, as well as the supposed personal, religious and political freedom in a "new" land, helped draw settlers to the West. As they moved, and eventually sought to set up new states, the question of whether such states would be admitted to the Union as free or slave threatened to disrupt the "balance" of free and slave states that had existed since 1820. Such problems could be dealt with by Congress, but the thought that one side or the other could, by adding a slave or free state, gain a majority in Congress, and thereby force their will on the entire country, alarmed abolitionists as well as slaveholders. The Congress had outlawed the Slave Trade itself in 1808, and, in 1820, declared the illegal slave trade a form of piracy punishable by death. There seemed to be common sentiment that slavery was not altogether noble or good. By the mid-Nineteenth century, however, Congress was becoming a battleground for those who wanted slavery abolished completely, and those who now saw slavery as a good and necessary institution for their way of life and that of black American slaves as well.

In the South, after a rejection of the colonization effort by Virginia in 1832, more and more people began to find positive arguments for slavery. Slavery, from this perspective, was no longer an old, unfortunate institution that had to be preserved as an heirloom of antiquity. Instead, supporters of slavery looked to the Bible, Aristotle, the Founding Fathers, and other sources of authority to actively promote slavery. In the Old Testament, they found examples of slavery. They pointed out passages that advised escaped slaves to return to their masters, and noted that Jesus did not advocate for an end to slavery. Supporters also played on popular prejudice and ethnocentrism to argue that black Americans were inferior and childlike, needing the direction and command of white Americans. In addition, they argued that slavery was profitable and necessary not just for the economy, but for social stability: given their understandable resentment for past treatment, freed black Americans could not be expected to live in harmony with white Americans, and would, instead, act in violence leading to racial wars. John C. Calhoun, the senator from South Carolina, argued that slavery gave many white Americans freedom from toil and drudgery, enabling them to study intellectual and practical matters of higher importance, much as was the case in the democracy of ancient Athens.

Anti- and Pro-Slavery convictions were also affected by the geographic expansion of America. While there were already conflicts about the hunting of fugitive slaves in the North, the possibility of new territories and states led to further debate over where slavery would be permitted or outlawed, and who had the right to make such decisions. While the question of the rights of native Americans, and treaties with native tribes, would be overlooked (as they are overlooked even today), the rights of settlers to continue to own slaves, and the rights of other settlers to vote to abolish slavery would be debated more and more fiercely. Pro-slavery forces saw the denial of slavery to settlers as a violation of 'protection of property' in the Fifth Amendment of the Constitution. Anti-slavery forces argued for the rights of settlers to determine whether or not they would allow slavery, and argued against the idea that people should be considered property in the first place.

The issue became politically prominent during the fighting of the Mexican War. Mexico, whose lands included much of what is now the western United States, had abolished slavery in its territory. So, anti-slavery politicians argued that when these lands became American, that abolition should continue. In 1846, in a famous amendment to a wartime, appropriations bill that President Polk had requested, David Wilmot of Pennsylvania stated that virtually all forms of slavery would be outlawed in lands the US might acquire from Mexico. The appropriations bill with this amendment, known as the Wilmot Proviso, was approved by the House, but not the Senate, and it was only after the President himself persuaded Wilmot to withdraw the amendment that he got his funds related to the war. But even though it did not become law, the Wilmot Proviso set off arguments that had been simmering for years since the Missouri Compromise. Calhoun and other Southern politicians argued that the debate over these issues might lead to disunion, and the fear of such disunion was an important influence on others in the debate. Senator Daniel Webster of Massachusetts, for instance, though representing a part of the country with support for the abolition of slavery, argued for a compromise in order to preserve the Union. That compromise, a set of five bills later called the Compromise of 1850, designated in which new states and territories slavery would be outlawed and in which places settlers could decide for themselves. But it also included a federal law, the Fugitive Slave Act.

While the Compromise of 1850 preserved the Union, though only for about a decade, the Fugitive Slave Act had broad consequences for life in the North. Provisions of the law denied a jury trial to those who were accused of being an escaped slave. The word of the slave-catcher was, apparently, to be trusted. This invited some to capture free black Americans, claim they were escaped slaves, and collect a fee for their troubles. The law also required citizens to aid in the capture of escaped slaves, regardless of their personal convictions, and threatened jail time and fines for those who did not comply. Northern intellectuals such as Ralph Waldo Emerson were indignant and advised people to openly break the law. At times, such as in October of 1850, in Detroit, the military had to be brought in to stop crowds of people from freeing someone who had been taken in as an escaped slave. So, the Compromise of 1850 was more of a veneer preserving the appearance of unity as the nation began to crack beneath its surface.

Dred Scott (1856)

As long as slavery stayed in the South, some Americans in the North were prepared to turn a blind-eye to the institution. As long as no one interfered with their practice of slavery, some Americans in the South were prepared to keep it to themselves as an important part of their heritage and economy. Politicians across the nation had been aware, for years, of the tension regarding slavery. They attempted to keep the issue at arm's length. Southern politicians had indirectly, and sometimes directly, warned of the danger of secession if they felt their way of life, which hinged on continuing slavery, was being threatened. This threat gave many politicians incentive to carefully avoid the issue when possible.

But the United States was one land with open borders between states. Not everyone was moving West. People also moved about the country for personal reasons, for economic reasons, and they took their property with them. Those who kept black Americans as slaves, and regarded them as property, moved about as well, and that movement crossed a line. The Fifth Amendment protected the right of private property, so people keeping slaves felt that the Constitution allowed for them to move with their slaves anywhere in the country. But that movement brought the practice of slavery into states in which that practice was considered illegal. Northerners who opposed slavery generally, though tolerated its existence in the Southern states, did not want to see it paraded in front of their noses in their own states. They had outlawed slavery, and numerous laws (Missouri Compromise, Compromise of 1850) had affirmed their "free" status. But now, they felt that their own laws were being made ineffectual when slave owners could freely bring enslaved black Americans to travel and live with them in Free states.

These tensions came to a head with the Supreme Court case of Dred Scott v. Sandford. Dred Scott, born around 1800, had been kept as a slave in Virginia, Alabama, and Missouri; all slave states. Around 1832, he was sold to a surgeon just entering service in the Army, John Emerson. Scott's status became curious, though not to his own knowledge, soon afterwards as Emerson was stationed at Rock Island in Illinois. Illinois was a free state in which slavery had been abolished. But Scott lived there with Emerson for roughly two years. Emerson was then ordered to Fort Snelling, in the Wisconsin territory, and Scott lived with him there for several years. Though not a state, the Wisconsin territory had been part of federal lands declared "free" by the Missouri Compromise legislation of 1820. So Scott (who by this time had married the slave of a local official near Fort Snelling, Harriet Robinson) had lived for about half a decade in lands which had been declared free of slavery by federal law. Emerson was stationed at various posts from St. Louis, to Louisiana to Florida, but Dred and Harriet were not told to follow him immediately, and spent time living with Emerson's new wife in St. Louis. Apparently, when summoned, they traveled down the Mississippi to meet up with the Emersons, on their own. After Emerson died in 1843, Dred was "loaned" out to one of Mrs. Emerson's relatives in the Army, which required him to move yet again, until he was sent back to Mrs. Emerson, and St. Louis, in 1846. He tried to buy freedom for himself and Harriet, for $300, but was turned down. Then, Dred Scott, perhaps with advice from the family of his former owner, went to court to try to secure his freedom.

His attorneys argued that because he and his wife had lived in a free state and a free territory, and not just traveled through these places, they had been emancipated. There had been a tacit agreement, earlier in the country's history, that slave owners would be allowed to travel through free states with their slaves. If the move became more permanent, however, it was understood that the slave would become free.

The details of the case, which began in 1847, are complicated, but after mixed decisions by lower courts, the Missouri State Supreme Court ruled against the Scotts. The attorneys decided it would be better to file a new case in a federal Circuit Court, this time against Mrs. Emerson's brother, John Sanford, who had assumed her legal defense when she moved to Massachusetts, and may have even become "owner" of the Scotts. That case began in 1854. But in order to bring that case, the attorneys had to assert that Dred Scott was a citizen. Sanford's attorney's claimed that he was not, and in the end the court decided in Sanford's favor. But the Supreme Court had recently found that corporations could bring cases to federal courts. In the 1844 case of Louisville, Cincinnati & Charleston R.R. v. Letson, the court had extended citizenship to corporations. If citizenship and its rights could be extended to corporations, then why not extend it to slaves as well? So Scott's attorney's appealed the case to the Supreme Court.

In 1856, when they heard Dred Scott's case, the Supreme Court was decidedly pro-South and pro-Slavery. In fact, five members came from families which held slaves. Arguing against Scott, Sanford's attorney's asserted that while Scott had lived in lands considered free, the laws that prohibited slavery in federal territory were unconstitutional.

In 1857, after postponing the case until after the contentious presidential election of 1856, the Court ruled against Dred Scott. Their main point, argued most forcefully by Chief Justice Taney, was that the Circuit Court had to dismiss the original case. Dred Scott was not a citizen, Taney argued, and therefore should not have been allowed to bring the case to federal court in the first place. So, on one level, dismissing the case meant that it should not have been argued in the first place, and the question about slavery in "free" lands should not have been asked.

But to reinforce the decision, Chief Justice Taney analyzed the claims about citizenship that the case had raised, and drew several important conclusions. Taney argued that there was nothing in the Constitution that gave Congress the power to grant citizenship to black Americans, nor that gave Congress the authority to empower territorial legislatures the power to do so. In this assertion, Taney linked free and enslaved, black Americans to the same status. Essentially, he contended that no black Americans, free or enslaved, could be considered citizens on the authority of the Constitution. In particularly strong language, he referred to all black

Americans as members of a subjugated race whose members had no rights because of past or present enslavement, whether it is that of themselves or their parents and grandparents. As such, the decision meant that the Missouri Compromise, a federal law, was now invalid.

Taney further analyzed the claim that Scott was free because he had lived in a free state. The State Supreme Court in Missouri had declared that Dred Scott was not a citizen, but a slave, regardless of the laws in other states or territories, and Taney affirmed that decision. So the laws of the state of residence when the case was filed took precedence over laws in the state in which Dred Scott had lived.

Taken together, the decision led many people in the North to fear that the Court, and other pro-Slavery political forces, would now extend slavery into the territories and perhaps into the "free" states themselves. This was an interpretation of the Constitution by the Supreme Court. Nothing short of amending the Constitution would change that interpretation, and such an amendment was impossible given the current political deadlock over slavery.

Civil War and Reconstruction

Those amendments would be possible, as it turned out, only after the Civil War. To be sure, there were other forces that played roles leading the Southern States to secede from the Union. But John Brown's raid on the federal arsenal at Harper's Ferry, Virginia, in 1859, along with his intent on fomenting insurrections of slaves across the South, was an important factor. While the raid itself ended in failure, investigations of Brown revealed he had correspondence with, and some support, from prominent abolitionists. Furthermore, the fact that anti-slavery leaders and spokespeople, such as Emerson and Garrison, openly considered Brown a martyr (he was hanged for the attack) gave leaders in the South plenty of reason to want to distance themselves from those in the North. Despite the platform that Abraham Lincoln ran on in 1860, which condemned Brown's raid and gave a nod to protecting state's rights, his election to the Presidency was seen as intolerable by many in the South. In December of 1860, South Carolina seceded from the Union, followed by six other Southern states in 1961.

Northern politicians tried to work out a compromise, starting just after the election in 1860. Led by Senator John Crittenden of Kentucky and Representative Thomas Corwin of Ohio, they argued various ideas, usually involving federal recognition of slavery in the South and defining precisely where it could be extended in the territories. Other Northern politicians, such as Lincoln, did not want recognition of slavery in the territories, but would allow such recognition where it existed at the time. Eventually, they were able to convince both the House and Senate (on a close vote) to pass a new Amendment to the Constitution which would explicitly recognize slavery as an institution of the South, but before the Amendment could be ratified by the states, the war intervened. The next time the country considered a 13th Amendment to the Constitution, it would be a very different document.

After the surrender of Fort Sumter in April of 1861, some, but not all, of the remaining slave states joined the Confederacy. In fact, the Western part of the state of Virginia split away and was eventually recognized by the Union as West Virginia. But the Civil War was a war between North and South, primarily. Lincoln, despite pressure from abolitionists, insisted that his first priority was the nation as a whole, not freeing slaves. There were still slave states in the Union. Lincoln had worked hard to keep them and didn't want to lose them. Nevertheless, as the war became bogged down and morale in the North dipped, Lincoln, asserting war powers, eventually signed the Emancipation Proclamation in 1863. The order freed slaves in most parts of the Confederacy, but in practice, most in the South (particularly black Americans) regarded it as freedom for all slaves in the Confederacy. But emancipation was not extended to slaves in Union lands, in large part because of resistance from the slave states that had remained in the Union. In addition to helping morale in the North, freeing slaves in the South would, it was believed, remove some of the labor power of the Confederacy, thereby helping the Northern strategy (nicknamed Anaconda by some) of strangling the Confederacy of resources that it needed to sustain itself.

Even during the war, Union forces had to decide what do with slaves freed by the war effort and by legislation directed at very specific parts of the country. Some black Americans, recently freed or escaped, served in the military. Soon, however, it became obvious that much more needed to be done for black American families. In 1865, the same year the Civil War ended, the Thirteenth Amendment was passed, outlawing slavery everywhere in the United States. Specifically, the Thirteenth Amendment provides in section 1: "Neither slavery nor involuntary servitude, except as a punishment for crime whereof the party shall have been duly convicted, shall exist within the United States, or any place subject to their jurisdiction."

While freedom was welcomed, black Americans were given little more. How could they survive without homes and a means to put food on the table? Slave owners had provided meager food and shelter; now they were free but left without either. Providing these basic necessities, however, would require land confiscations and distributions, and many people, even many abolitionists, balked at such radical changes in property ownership. Especially as confederate states were re-admitted to the Union, the question of the protection of private property in the Fifth Amendment was raised. In the end, though some politicians such as Charles Sumner of Massachusetts proposed establishing forty acre properties for freedmen, the only accommodations that were made were temporary ones, such as food distribution and some rented property which was administered by the newly created Freedman's Bureau.. The victorious Union wanted to reestablish itself, not reinvent itself.

At the end of the Civil War, political leaders needed to deal with how to treat the people of the defeated Confederacy. Were they still citizens of the United States with all of the same rights and protections, such as the right to vote and serve in Congress? Clearly, the Union did not want to return to a Congress like the one that had preceded the War.

After Lincoln's assassination, the succession to the Presidency of Andrew Jackson, himself a native of North Carolina who had served in Congress from Tennessee, and whose views seemed, increasingly, to favor the South, alarmed Northern politicians. While saying that those who had turned on the Union should suffer some punishment, Johnson issued over 13,000 special pardons. At one point, he vetoed a bill to continue funding the Freedman's Bureau, arguing that the bill was only a wartime measure (while the country had returned to peace) and that it had been approved by a Congress that didn't include eleven of the states. Furthermore, he argued that care for the homeless was not a power granted to Congress by the Constitution. While he was unpopular among Northern political leaders for these and other reasons, in some ways he was continuing policies that Lincoln had approved earlier. Both had advocated that former slave states only give suffrage to the most intelligent of black Americans as well as those who had served in the military. Also like Lincoln, Johnson had considered the Union as an indivisible entity. The states of the Confederacy had not really seceded; individuals in those states had, instead, broken federal laws. Now that the war had resolved things, it was only fitting to return to how things were, provided that political leaders in the South swore oaths and enacted the Thirteenth Amendment.

    Indeed, the eleven states that had been the Confederacy had formed state governments, and while paying lip-service to Johnson's requirements for re-admission, were carrying on business as usual. A number of former Confederate political and military leaders were even elected to Congress, though the Congress refused to seat them. How could it make sense that the results of a horrendously bloody war would allow for some of the very people who provoked the war to now be part of the government they had fought against. Furthermore, while they had freed the slaves in their states, the former Confederate states had begun to impose new laws, the Black Codes, which restricted and repressed black Americans in ways similar to that of slavery. While a few, restricted property rights were given, black Americans were required to sign yearly labor contracts. Black American children often had to be apprenticed to a "master" who could punish them physically if he felt it was called for. There were punishments and fines for vagrancy. Mississippi basically enacted a code that exchanged the words freedman for slaves, but otherwise treated them virtually the same. Many Republican Congressmen, led by Representative Thaddeus Stevens of Pennsylvania and Senator Charles Sumner of Massachusetts, became more convinced that reconstruction was necessary. A radical changed needed to be made in the South. Against Johnson's understanding of secession, the Radical Republicans asserted that the former Confederate states had lost all important civil and political rights because they had seceded, and that Congress had the authority to impose requirements for regaining those rights.

    Against President Johnson's will, and overriding his veto in both cases, Congress passed a new Freedman's Bureau bill, as well as a Civil Rights Act. The Civil Rights Act of 1866 acted against the Black Codes of various states by asserting that everyone who was born in the United States, other than Indians, was a citizen with the same rights and benefits accorded by the law. To bolster this Act, which Johnson believed was unconstitutional, Congress enacted the Fourteenth Amendment, which was later ratified in 1868.

    The Fourteenth Amendment, passed in 1866 and ratified by 1868, made several changes and clarifications which were meant to bring about more equity in how black and white Americans were treated and protected by the law of the land. It explicitly stated that any person born or naturalized in the United States was considered a citizen by federal and state governments, and was therefore guaranteed equal rights and protections under the law. States were not permitted to make or enforce laws which acted against any person's lawful "privileges or immunities," nor deprive them of "life, liberty or property" without "due process of law." The

Amendment also changed the way representation would be determined for the House of Representatives by asserting that only the number of whole persons would be counted toward figuring the number of representatives accorded. This removed the "three-fifths" clause in Article One of the Constitution, which had counted each slave as three-fifths of a person for figuring out representation. The Amendment also stated that if the right to vote were denied to any male person, other than non-taxed Indians, those persons excluded would not be counted toward figuring representation in Congress. This "punishment" for denying the right to vote was fairly specific, but not overly punitive, and the Amendment also included a section stating that Congress could pass further legislation spelling out rules for enforcing the specifics of this Amendment.

On the one hand, the language of the Amendment seems specific enough, e.g.: "All persons born or naturalized in the United States, and subject to the jurisdiction thereof, are citizens of the United States and of the State wherein they reside. No State shall make or enforce any law which shall abridge the privileges or immunities of citizens of the United States; nor shall any State deprive any person of life, liberty, or property, without due process of law; nor deny to any person within its jurisdiction the equal protection of the laws." On the other hand, in future decisions, that specificity would be challenged. In the *Slaughterhouse Cases* (1873) the Supreme Court held that the Fourteenth Amendment provides freed slaves only with the rights related to national citizenship, not those related to citizenship as defined by the states.

In theory, the Fifteenth Amendment protected the right to vote more explicitly by stating that it could not be "denied or abridged" by the federal or any state government, "on account of race, color, or previous condition of servitude." Given the fact that black Americans had been denied the right of vote, among other things, this Amendment seemed to be directed at assuring that black Americans, as well as white Americans, could vote in federal and state elections. But in practice, that was far from the case. Suffrage, the right to vote, had been limited in numerous ways from early on in the nation's government. It was not until the mid-nineteenth century that most states removed the property requirements which had limited suffrage to the more wealthy citizens of the country. Apart from a very brief period of time in New Jersey, women (propertied or not) had never enjoyed suffrage. Indeed, even Republicans such as Lincoln did not want suffrage extended to all black Americans, but only to those who were intelligent or had served in the military. People in power did not have trust that everyone's character and intelligence would be high enough to govern well. So, while the Fifteenth Amendment served as a basis for black American suffrage and participation in state and federal government, it had to be supported and enforced in many parts of the South, or it would not have happened.

The long history of slavery, segregation and, finally, desegregation cannot be fully understood without examining the role of law in American life. It is a history of battles to subjugate people with the status of property, as well as battles for rights, freedom and equality, fought out on the pages of law books and on the floors of courtrooms over many years.

Though a number of African-Americans enjoyed relative equality with whites in the 17th century English colonies, by the 18th century most had been thoroughly subordinated, even the free black people of the Northern colonies. The new status of

African-Americans was enshrined in the United States Constitution, which allowed the slave trade to continue and required runaway slaves to be returned to their masters. By 1856, the United States Supreme Court could declare that people of the African race had "no rights a white man was bound to respect"[8].

The Amendments gave Congress the power to pass legislation to ensure their protections to the freed slaves. The Civil Rights Acts of 1866, 1870, 1871, and 1875 were the first legislative attempts to assure African Americans an equal political and legal status. These Civil Rights Acts were in direct response to the Black Codes (the South's answer to Emancipation and the Thirteenth Amendment). The Civil Rights Acts nullified most of the restrictions the Black Codes placed upon the freed former slaves.

The 1866 Act confirmed African American's status as citizens, their right to sue in court, to engage in contracts, and to hold and deal in property (real and personal). The 1866 Act is still good law, and is presently codified in the United States Code as 42 USC 1981 and 1982.

In response to terrorist attacks upon freed slaves by organizations such as the Ku Klux Klan, Congress passed a series of bills called "Enforcement Acts" to prevent violence and intimidation against individuals attempting to exercise their constitutional rights. One of these Acts was passed in 1870 (now codified as 42 USC 1971) and two in 1871 (one has since been repealed; the other is presently codified at 42 USCA 1983).

A key focal point of the 1870 Act was the right to vote, and the misuse of one's position as an election officer to inhibit the right to vote. This aspect of the Enforcement Acts was eviscerated by the Supreme Court in *U.S. v Reese* (1875), which dismissed an indictment against inspectors of elections that refused to *count* the votes of a black person, on the grounds that the statute, and the Fifteenth Amendment, only spoke to *preventing* blacks from voting! Though direct voter intimidation by public officials was unconstitutional and illegal, election fraud was not. And, of course, if any private citizen wanted to intimidate blacks in the exercise of the franchise, that did not constitute "state action" and so, could not be redressed by Congress, per the *Civil Rights Cases*.

In *US v. Cruikshank* (1875), the US Supreme Court dismissed an indictment brought under the 1871 Act against a mob of whites who murdered more than one hundred black people, because the Fourteenth Amendment gave Congress power only over state action, and not the acts of individuals, per the *Civil Rights Cases*. Thus the Enforcement Acts, which were passed to stem Ku Klux Klan activity, could not be used to indict members of the Klan.

The 1875 Act secured equal access to public accommodations, ands prohibited exclusion of blacks from jury duty. The 1875 Act was overturned by the Supreme Court in the *Civil Rights Cases* (1883), on the ground that the Fourteenth Amendment gave Congress jurisdiction over units of government only, and not private persons. Thus, an individual might discriminate in a restaurant or hotel against a black person, so long as the government was not directly involved.

---

[8] Dred Scott v. Sanford, 60 U.S. 393 (1857)

Support for black American suffrage also came in the form of efforts to inform black Americans, as well as loyal white Southerners, of their rights, and encourage participation in government. Members of the Union League, a nationalist organization that began in 1862, worked to promote patriotism and democratic participation in government. While white Southerners still managed to hold many positions in government during the Reconstruction period, there were black American representatives in state governments, as well as very modest representation in Congress: two senators and fourteen members of the House.

Reconstruction itself was an effort, led by Congressional Republican politicians, to combat Southern resistance to the end of slavery and to equal rights with black Americans. While President Johnson led reconciliation meetings, symbolizing the re-union of Americans, North and South, Republicans such as Thaddeus Stevens and Charles Sumner worked within the Joint Committee on Reconstruction to ensure that re-union meant something more than merely returning to the way things were before the war. White Americans in the South still held virtually the same beliefs and desires for how life ought to be lived and how society ought to be organized, as they did before the war. If the North had really been victorious, however, and if some future confrontation was to be averted, those beliefs and desires, and the practices that followed from them, had to change.

The Reconstruction Committee operated with the understanding that the states which had joined the Confederacy had given up a number of the civil and political rights that they had enjoyed under the Constitution, and that Congress had the authority to dictate the changes that these states would have to make a reality before they could be granted those rights back. Federal troops and military governments would help protect black Americans, and white Republicans, in the South for the time being, making sure that new laws protecting them were being enforced. The Military Reconstruction Act, as it had been originally conceived, would have put all law enforcement in the former Confederate states in the hands of the federal military in order to ensure that new laws were enforced. It was also meant to extend authorization of military rule as long as necessary. More moderate and conciliatory voices amended the Act (the Blaine amendment) so that the Act, passed over President Johnson's veto in 1867, required the states to ratify the Fourteenth Amendment, as well as acknowledge the right of black Americans to vote, but not much more. It did authorize military commanders to 'keep the peace' and protect the rights and property of all. It also authorized the use of military tribunals, rather than civil courts, when necessary. The Republicans did not trust local law enforcement, nor juries composed of white Southerners whose views on black Americans had changed little if at all since the War. Two other Reconstruction Acts were passed later that year to require the military to take a more active role in getting all men of voting age (black or white) registered to vote, as well as to remove former officials in the Confederacy from office.

So, Reconstruction was an active and fairly forceful effort to change the political landscape, and thereby the cultural landscape, of the states that had been slave states of the Confederacy. For a number of years, it seemed to have some effect. When the Georgia state legislature removed black Americans who had been elected to office, the admission of Georgia back into the Union was withdrawn, the black American representatives were allowed their seats, and known Confederates were removed from the legislature. When the terrorist activities of the Ku Klux Klan against black Americans intensified, further measures were passed allowing for group arrests and suspension of the writ of habeas corpus.

For a time, such measures seemed to be holding white terrorism in check. But it was clear that the presence of the military governments and federal troops continued to be necessary to carry out Reconstruction. White Southerners were not "warming up" to the idea of equality with black Americans; they were trying to find ways to try to discourage black Americans from seeking their rights.

End of Reconstruction and the Compromise of 1877

For some political leaders, the Reconstruction effort may have been less about black American suffrage and equality, and more about punishing those who were seen as traitors to the nation. As victors of the Civil War, they wanted to ensure domination of the nation's political life over those who had lost the war. President Johnson's efforts to thwart many of the Reconstruction measures also drove more moderate politicians to support policies of the Radical Republicans. But during the Grant Presidency, that support faded as the Reconstruction effort became more and more burdensome. There was quite a bit of corruption within the administration involving the misuse of public funds which ended up in private hands. Corruption was not limited to Republicans, but the fact of corruption was a problem that required attention. Desires for further expansion of the nation geographically, as wells concerns about wars with Indians, sapped much of the missionary zeal that had surrounded some of the efforts at Reconstruction in the South.

While the military could hunt down the Ku Klux Klan and other terrorist groups, some Southern politicians realized that fighting those troops directly would not be necessary if other means could be used to have them removed from the South. The opportunity came in the Presidential election of 1876. In the initial counting of electoral votes, the Democrat, Tilden, had more than the Republican, Hayes. But Tilden was one vote short of the required 185 electors necessary to win the Presidency. Neither candidate had 185 because a number of the votes were in dispute; there had been a good bit of voter fraud and practices to discourage others from voting. Congress, which was divided between a Democratic House and Republican Senate, was not able to find a way to decide the election. Eventually, they established an Electoral Commission to get to the bottom of things. While this commission may have attempted to discern who really won the election, it is now clear that the result was only agreed upon by a majority of Congress after politicians struck a deal, the Compromise of 1877. Democrats would give up claim on the disputed electoral votes, making Hayes President, as long as Hayes promised to removed federal troops from the several places they were still stationed in the South. Hayes also would promise to support several transportation-related projects in the South, while Democrats would support the Civil War Amendments. There were several other agreements as well, but these latter agreements were largely ignored by other sides once Hayes was President and the former Confederate states were not under the rule of the federal military. The North could feel satisfied that, at least on paper, its sense of morality had triumphed, and now they didn't have to spend so much time and effort governing others. The South could swallow its pride and accept the laws as words on paper, while enjoying the fact that they were now allowed to rule themselves without outside interference. Indeed, the protections for black American's rights and general well-being were slowly eroded, both by Supreme Court interpretations, as well as by the actions and inactions of local and state law enforcement throughout the South.

While slavery had existed in the South, there had been segregation in the North since before the Civil War. Indeed, it could be said that there was a fair amount of hypocrisy in Northern ambitions to reconstruct the South, when race relations were far from equitable in the North itself. One of the more famous examples of the strains between black and white Americans in the North was the move to enforce segregation in schooling in Connecticut, particularly the case of Prudence Crandall and her private school for girls. Crandall, a Quaker who was originally from Rhode Island, was successfully running a private, girls' school early in the 1830s in Connecticut, until she admitted a black American girl. White American parents complained and pulled their daughters from the school, but Crandall did not give in to pressure to keep her school White-only until 1833 when she opened a school for black American girls in the same town; Canterbury. This concession to a version of "separate, but equal" did not, however, satisfy many of the white citizens of Connecticut, who tried to stop supplies from getting to the school and also tried to burn the school building down. Local officials tried to use vagrancy laws to threaten the students' with whippings if they attended. Then, in 1834, Connecticut passed a law outlawing free schools for black American girls. Crandall continued her school anyway and was arrested and throw in jail. When she won her appeal of the case, an enraged mob of local white citizens threatened both the school, and Crandall and her students, with physical harm. Crandall decided that it was better to move away, out of concern for the well-being of her students.

Connecticut was not a slave state, to be sure, but this incident was typical of the intolerant and viscous attitude that haunted community relations in the North. There had been economic segregation, of course, for some time; some parts of a train or theater were reserved for higher-paying customers. While some restaurants, theaters, and railways accepted wealthier black Americans into the first-class areas, however, others did not, and required them to be seated in second-class or smoking cars and accommodations. There were also some businesses, both in the North and the West of the country, which did not serve black Americans on any terms. Indeed, there were a number of law suits after passage of the Civil Rights Act of 1866, in cities such as Boston and Baltimore and for a train that ran between New York and Washington. But the legal teeth of the law did not scare people who did not want to have to associate with black Americans. In 1871, for instance, a black passenger on a streetcar in Louisville, Kentucky won a suit against the company for being forced off the streetcar after sitting inside the car, instead of out on the platform, which was where black Americans were assigned. When other black passengers attempted to sit inside the cars after hearing about this verdict, mobs of white Americans, unhindered by local police, harassed them verbally and physically. Finally, after they attempted to fight back, the black passengers were arrested for disorderly conduct. Other white mobs led similar attacks in the days that followed. Local courts took the liberty of defending the arrests on the assertion that the Civil Rights law was, in their opinion, unconstitutional.

The Fourteenth Amendment was the subject of a series of cases which undercut and eventually dismantled Reconstruction in the legal arena. The Supreme Court in the *Civil Rights Cases* (1883) upheld the Civil Rights Acts insofar as they prohibited discrimination that was the product of governmental action. The Court held, however, that the equal protection clause of the 14th Amendment did not prohibit private acts of discrimination. Thus it overturned the Civil Rights Act of 1875, which prohibited innkeepers, proprietors of public establishments, and owners of public conveyances from discriminating against African Americans in public accommodations. The *Civil Rights Cases* held that Congress was powerless to remedy discrimination by one individual against another individual. Congress could only prevent action taken by states that deprived their citizens of constitutionally-granted rights. Moreover, citizens had to first turn to their states to challenge the deprivation, and only when the state failed to act, could the Federal branches step in. This requirement is referred to as "state action" and despite forceful arguments against "state action," it remains a court-imposed requirement for individuals who wish to challenge denial of their civil rights under the Constitution.

Justice John Marshall Harlan, in a vigorous dissent, argued that the Court's action basically revived the odious *Dred Scott* opinion's disregard for the rights of African-Americans. Harlan also dissented in *Plessy v. Ferguson*.

Plessy v. Ferguson (1896)

Passage of the Civil Rights Act of 1875, a federal law similar in spirit to the earlier Civil Rights Act, seemingly guaranteed that black Americans would have freedom from discrimination and equal access to "accommodations, advantages, facilities, and privileges of inns, public conveyances on land or water, theaters, and other places of public amusement." As test cases reached the Supreme Court in 1883, however, the Justices all but unanimously ruled the Act unconstitutional. They argued that the Fourteenth Amendment had, quite literally, forbade any *state* from denying citizens equal protection under the law, but that was all. The Amendment, by their "strict construction" reading, did not apply to individuals or companies; it only applied to states. So, private individuals and private companies could not be stopped from treating black and white Americans differently.

One of the Justices, Joseph Bradley, had implied that the War Amendments to the Constitution had given black Americans special rights and privileges, which, while necessary at the time to help former slaves, could not be understood to last forever. The intent of the Amendments, he argued, was not to 'play favorites' forever, but to give temporary, legal help only. His view seemed to echo that of many politicians, especially in the South. The freedom of individuals and companies to decide seating policies would no longer be curtailed; from their point of view, that 'special privilege' benefiting black Americans was over.

But during the 1880s, there was still a good bit of interaction between white and black Americans. In South Carolina and Louisiana, there were some railroads, eating and drinking establishments, theaters and other public places which did not separate white and black

Americans. The courts had declared that individuals and companies could discriminate, but had not mandated that they should. Legislatures, however, slowly took that next step toward requiring segregation. Some white Americans believed that the nature of black Americans was different from their own. They believed that interaction between white and black people, especially between people of different genders, was inspired only by a desire for illicit behavior. They also believed that without the limitations that slavery had imposed, black Americans would naturally "regress" to a beast-like state, and therefore be a danger to white Americans. Cultural differences were exaggerated and manipulated. In some ways, it was the imagination of these white Americans which had "regressed" and become wild. But as fear and ignorance mounted, between 1881 and 1890, states began to pass legislation that required separation of passengers on the basis of race. The case of Plessy v. Ferguson (1898) challenged this unofficial policy.

Black Americans, of course, could see the writing on the wall, and acted vigorously to try to stop the tide of change. In 1890, when a railroad segregation bill was introduced in the Louisiana State Legislature, a well-educated group of black Americans in New Orleans organized to oppose it. For a time, they succeeded, with the help of some black legislators, in slowing the bill's progress. Later in the year, however, the bill was passed and signed into law. One of the members of the group, Rudolphe Desdunes, suggested a boycott of the railroads, and it was considered.

But in the end, they followed the suggestion of Louis Martinet, a young lawyer in the group, who argued for testing the constitutionality of the new law in court. They raised money in preparation for a legal battle, and even hired a prominent, New York lawyer who had been a force in the reconstruction effort in North Carolina after the war, as their primary counsel. Railroad officials, some of whom disliked the new law because of the cost required to supply extra cars and were not enforcing it, agree to help "stage" a direct act of disobedience to the law. The first test case was a successful failure. It was successful, in that they won the case, but unsuccessful in that the law was not judged wholly unconstitutional in the process. The test traveler had a ticket to go to Alabama, outside the state, and the court held that the railroad law was unconstitutional only as it applied to people traveling between states. The Supreme Court had given sole authority to regulate interstate commerce to Congress. But regulation of commerce within a state was not restricted, nor had that been specifically challenged by the test case because the ticket had been an interstate ticket. The victory was hollow since the states around Louisiana had similar segregation laws for travel within their states. It was still virtually impossible for black Americans to avoid segregation in railroad travel. The next time they planned a test; the traveler, Homer Plessy, purchased a ticket to travel within the state only. When he was arrested, they had the case they wanted.

Martinet and his lawyers lost their first case regarding the constitutionality of the railroad segregation law before a judge in New Orleans, John Ferguson. They appeal to the State Supreme Court, which found that the law which required "separate, but equal" accommodations did not violate the Fourteenth Amendment. The Chief Justice, Francis Nicholls, was the former Louisiana Governor who had signed the railroad segregation law just a few years earlier. Ironically, when he had first become governor in 1877, he had opposed discrimination, given some state office to black Americans, and had acted to protect them. But with the rise of Populism, he and other conservative politicians had sought to drive a wedge between white and black Americans, many of whom had been united in Populist causes. Since the 1880s, the Populist movement had worked to help farmers avoid an industry of middlemen and get their crops directly to people, to the economic advantage of both. They had advocated the direct election of senators, government control of the transportation industry, and changes in the monetary policy to help debt-laden farmers who had suffered in the post-War period of deflation. Especially after the general strike which paralyzed New Orleans in 1892, many white conservatives were ready to break up the Populist movement by playing the racial card.

So, after their appeal was turned down by the State Supreme Court, lawyers for the New Orleans group managed to get the case accepted by the United State Supreme Court, which heard it in 1895, after a three-year delay. More than one argument was advanced, but the more substantial objection was that the segregation law could not be reconciled with the Thirteenth and Fourteenth Amendments. The law's purpose, it was argued, was to institute a subservient status for black Americans, not just a different status as the "separate, but equal" argument implied. They pointed out that the law made an exception for black nurses serving white children. Thus, as long as black Americans played the role of a servant, they could share accommodations with white Americans. If they played the role of an independent and equal citizen, they had to go to a different car. The intent of such a visible separation was to strengthen the view that black Americans were inferior to white Americans.

By a wide margin, the Court disagreed. Writing the opinion of the Court, Justice Henry Brown, citing precedent as well as common practice at the time, argued that segregation laws were 'reasonable' and did not violate the Thirteenth or Fourteenth Amendments. Brown asserted that a 'reasonable' law is one that a legislature has found to be in accord with advancing peaceful conduct and comfortable relations in society, given the traditional practices and customs of that society. The Thirteenth and Fourteenth Amendments were not intended to change the culture of society, but only to protect the political equality of the people generally. In effect, Brown argued that political rights could be protected without any change in the customs and culture of society generally. In reference to the view of former Chief Justice Shaw, in 1849, Brown asserted that the law neither causes, nor cures, prejudice. Segregation of black and white Americans, by this argument, reasonably promoted peace in the present society, and did not infringe on political equality in the least.

In effect, the Court said that the Fourteenth Amendment's purpose was to equalize the treatment of blacks and whites, but that "it could not have been intended to abolish distinctions based upon color, or to enforce social, as distinguished from political
equality, or a commingling of the two races upon terms unsatisfactory to either." Thus the US Supreme Court gave its stamp of approval to segregation under the specious doctrine of "separate but equal," facilitating an era of "separate but equal" laws which survived in various forms until 1967.

Justice Brown's views may have seemed 'reasonable' to some living in his time, given the success of fear mongering, and given the rash of lynching and mob violence that was occurring in the 1890s. But this line of thinking also suggests that just because members of one group cannot live peacefully in the presence of another group which asserts its equality, that both groups must be separated. The intolerant customs and attitudes of members of one group (and, to be sure, not every white American felt a need for segregation) were to be respected, and could not be understood to affect anyone outside that group. Brown argued that if black Americans felt inferior by being required to travel in separate cars, then they were the ones who made themselves feel inferior. He further implied that black Americans were, indeed, *socially* inferior; but that just as the law could not change the physical appearance of people, it could not change their social status either. He applied this not merely to state and federal laws, but to the Constitution itself. The War Amendments, and presumably future Amendments, could mandate political equality, but could not enforce social equality. There was only so much that law could do.

Segregation (Jim Crow Laws)

Of course, the upshot of the *Plessy v. Ferguson* decision was that it emboldened segregationists to pass more and more legislation aimed at separating black and white Americans from one another. While the law could not, as Justice Brown argued, change people's customs and prejudices, the decision of the Court did, in fact, alter and give a kind of respect to the tradition of prejudice. People who found such a separation distasteful to their cultural sentiments had to endure segregation. Their traditional ways were not, it seemed, as important as those which saw the interaction of black and white Americans as distasteful and dangerous. In his dissent, Justice Marshall Harlan predicted that the decision, that these segregation laws did not violate the War Amendments, would lead to further, and sometimes brutal, assaults on the rights of black Americans.

Segregation Laws, referred to as Jim Crow Laws (after a character in the blackface minstrel shows in the mid-19th century) came to define and restrict more and more aspects of daily life in the states that enacted them. There were laws that segregated trains and other forms of public transportation. Laws were enacted regarding hospitals, 'protecting' white nurses from being asked to attend to black patients. Hotels and restaurants were segregated, as well as buses, swimming pools, billiard halls, rest rooms, community parks, and even cemeteries. Louisiana passed a law trying to segregate circuses by requiring separate ticket booths a specific distance apart. White Americans and black Americans could not play baseball within two blocks of one another, in Georgia. Georgia also made sure there would be no black barbers cutting the hair of white women. Indeed, the stereotype of black men possessing inferior and suspect character was, very likely, behind some of these laws that specifically mentioned black men and white women. Marriage was also segregated; Arizona, Georgia and Maryland, among others, passed intermarriage laws which would not allow white Americans to marry members of a variety of ethnic groups. Schools, even those for the mentally challenged and for the blind, were also required by many states to be segregated.

Plessy specifically approved separate "but equal" schools for black children as constitutional.[9] However, when African-American children attended school at all, they did so in separate schools which were inferior in virtually every respect to those of white children, save for the dedication of their teachers. Poorly maintained, crumbling, often with no indoor plumbing, and located far away from the homes of many children (for whom no buses were provided) the notion that Jim Crow segregated schools were "equal" as well as separate seems to have been some kind of cruel joke.

If segregation laws were 'reasonable' because they were intended to keep peaceful relations between black and white Americans, as Justice Brown had argued, they were a failure at keeping the peace for black Americans. Lynchings in the 1890s averaged about 188 a year. If they were not an infringement on political equality, but only an expression of the 'obvious' social inequality, they were a failure as well. The cultural tradition that Jim Crow sprang from was not content with merely emphasizing and maintaining social differences; it feared the political power of black voters and moved to neutralize them. Politicians, in the South especially, passed legislation which effectively took suffrage away from black Americans, while preserving it for most white Americans.

Disfranchisement of black American men followed a pattern set by Mississippi. One element was a residency requirement, which was difficult for black American tenant farmers and migrant workers to establish since they moved frequently in search of better jobs. A second element was the disqualification of voters who had committed crimes. Given all of the segregation laws and the fact that law enforcement was primarily white, it was not difficult to find ways to charge black Americans with 'crimes.' Poll taxes were required, and often had to be paid many months before the election. A poor person who could afford the tax then had to keep his receipt safe for months, so he could present it and be allowed to vote. The fourth aspect of this process was the literacy requirement. Literacy was not uncommon to white or black Americans, especially the poor. The white politicians did not want to lose, or anger, white voters, so they included a number of loopholes in the law: if the registrar deemed that a voter could understand the Constitution, despite being unable to read it, that voter could be allowed to vote. Also, if a voter's father or grandfather had been eligible to vote in 1867 (before black Americans were allowed to vote) they could be "grandfathered" and allowed to vote. The overall effect was to decimate the black vote, though it was done in a way that was indirect enough, by a strict reading of the law, to avoid being deemed unconstitutional.

As the segregation laws crept into more and more aspects of daily life, it became important for some to better define who was, and who was not, "black." While laws against marriage between "whites and "blacks" existed, there was a long history of children being born from one parent of African ancestry and the other of European ancestry. In Latin America, and parts of the American South, there had been a higher social status for people depending on the degree to which they could claim European ancestry. Terms like mulatto, quadroon and octoroon were used in conversation to distinguish degrees of European ancestry, with higher status and privilege being accorded to those with more European ancestry. During the Jim Crow period, segregation laws often contained this language, but its use was guided by what came to

---

[9] *Plessy v. Ferguson*, 163 U.S. 537,544 (1896)

be know as the "one-drop rule." According to the "one-drop rule," a person was regarded as "black" for the purpose of segregation, so long as they had any African ancestry at all. The pseudo-science of the day suggested that there was a difference in people's blood, depending on the continent of their ancestors, and apparently even one drop of African blood could not be diluted. Virginia went so far as to pass legislation outlawing marriage between white Americans and anyone with even a trace of African "blood." Other states would allow marriage if the person marrying a white American had 1/8th African ancestry or less. While pernicious, the one-drop rule was also often difficult to enforce, since people of mixed ancestry could sometimes "pass" for white, among people who did not know their family history.

Part of the legacy of segregation is the difficulty people in the United States have had in agreeing on terminology with regard to ancestry. As mentioned, those who opposed early 19th century colonization efforts often distanced themselves from the terms African or African-American. During the Jim Crow period, terms such as "black," "negro" and "colored" were used. Later in the mid-20th century, "Afro-American" and finally "African-American" became more acceptable. There are various reasons and histories behind these terms, and we will not discuss them in detail at present. We have been using the term "black-American" up to this point in the exposition of history leading up to the Civil Rights Movement. While it is somewhat arbitrary to shift at this point, as opposed to another, we will now use the more currently acceptable term "African-American" instead of "black American." We will also use similar, hyphenated-terms, such as "European-American" or "Asian-American" when necessary, with the caveat that terminology has been, and will continue to be, inadequate to fully express truth and beauty in humanity.

Before the first World War, African-Americans faced a country which, North and South, did not have a great interest in protecting their rights or advancing the quality of their lives. Nevertheless, they found a variety of ways to continue the struggle, despite obstacles. One way was to foster a sense of community among other African-Americans. Newspapers owned and run by African-Americans responded to the need for closer ties and a better sense of what was being done to African-Americans than the traditional press cared to discuss. In the 1890s, there were hundreds of "black" newspapers. In addition to functioning as a forum for community discussion, many helped advance the view that through self-reliance and hard work, African-Americans could work within "the system" of segregation, and improve their quality of life. This view echoed that of Booker T. Washington, founder of the Tuskegee Institute in Alabama, who had encouraged African-Americans to train for the kind of jobs that segregation allowed. His apolitical stance was opposed by many, prominent African-American leaders, such as W.E.B. DuBois, who argued for a more liberal education and a more politically astute and active community. DuBois and others were part of the Niagara Movement and, a few years later in 1910, the National Association for the Advancement of Colored People (NAACP). These groups worked to publicize the ugly side of segregation (e.g. lynchings, voter fraud) which, they felt, Washington and European-American society wanted to overlook and tolerate.

African-Americans with the desire and resources for a good education were confronted by the reality that "separate but equal" almost never meant equal. Public schools for African-

American children often under-funded in comparison to schools for European-American nearby. Facilities, supplies and teacher salaries at schools for African-Americans all suffered because of this inequality. The schools were regarded as "equal," however, by the political establishment which sought to conform, in name, to the Plessy v. Ferguson verdict mandating separate but equal treatment for African-Americans and European-Americans.

This separation continued into higher education. While the Morrill Act of 1890 aimed to help African-American students by asserting that states would not receive federal funding for their agricultural and mechanical colleges unless they provided similar schools for African-Americans, the Act corresponded with the "separate but equal" doctrine and helped increase the number of "black" colleges.

Many of these schools focused on practical skills and training, as opposed to a more liberal arts education, and this was not by accident. Advocates of segregation advanced the pseudo-scientific view that African-Americans were inferior to European-Americans, both morally and intellectually. Educational facilities needed to be separate to avoid the moral corruption they believe would result from interaction between European-American and African-American students. Furthermore, they believed that African-Americans were not intellectual able to learn, nor to be trusted with, anything more than a technical education, in a skill that could earn them a modest living. Thus, education was separate, but "equal" only for students seeking the more technical kinds of training.

Wartime segregation

While the Jim Crow laws would continue in the 20th century, the advent of the first World War brought changes to the lives of African-Americans. While some had fled to the North to escape slavery, during the days of the "underground railroad," there were many African-Americans who began to move North for economic security. The hardships of sharecropping combined with the treatment they experienced under the Jim Crow laws created a desire for a better place to work and live, and the need for workers in factories of the Northern industrial centers, especially after the US entry into the first World War, provided a way to satisfy that desire.

During the first World War, African-Americans served in segregated units. European-American soldiers often expressed surprise that the African-American soldiers fought as well and as bravely as they did. What they had expected was consistent with the view that African-Americans lacked the same moral character and intellectual ability of European-Americans, that developed alongside segregation. Nevertheless, American soldiers, regardless of their ancestry, demonstrated their equality on the battlefield. Many African-American soldiers believed that the quality of their service be proof enough of equality, and would lead to a difference in treatment after the war.

African-Americans serving in WWI, however, came home to ignorance and fear, rather than patriotic gratitude. Though they had served their country, some European-Americans convinced themselves that these soldiers had interacted with people in Europe (particularly 'white' European women and 'red' Communist European men) enough to develop bad habits and beliefs that they would now bring back to America. The smallest accusation of European-American woman having a romantic relationship with an African-American man could touch off a race riot, as it did in Longview, Texas in 1919. The effort of African-Americans to form a union in their line of work could do the same, as it did in Elaine, Arkansas, in the same year. In Chicago and Washington, and a score of other places, officials struggled to contain the violence of race riots.

Segregation in civilian life, as well as in the military, continued through the years between the Wars. African-American lawyers, who had found ways to get more than the technical education that segregationist society thought was "fit" for them, pressed for true equality through the courts. In the 1930s, the NAACP, with the legal leadership of Charles Hamilton Houston, brought cases forward in an effort to challenge the "separate but equal" basis for segregation. Houston and other African-American lawyers, such as Thurgood Marshall, strategically decided to advance cases challenging segregation in graduate and law school education, in part because they sensed less resistance to it from the contemporary culture of the South. While the integrated schooling of young children was deemed dangerous from a moral standpoint, by segregationists, they were less worried about such integration in higher education. Perhaps they felt that younger children were less set in their ways and habits, and hence had to be "protected."

One of the first victories for this strategy came in 1938 with the Supreme Court decision of Missouri ex rel Gaines v. Canada. Lloyd Gaines had applied to the University of Missouri School of Law and, though qualified, was denied because he was African-American. Missouri law allowed that people in his situation could be offered scholarships to attend law school in another state. Indeed, this was the practice of a number of Southern states. The Court, however, decided in favor of the arguments of Houston and the NAACP that the privilege of attending law school in one's own state had been violated by this practice and was unconstitutional under the "equal protection" clause of the 14th Amendment. Other victories, such as the 1948 Sipuel v. Board of Regents decision and the 1950 Sweatt v. Painter decision, would move closer and closer to a direct challenge of the Plessy "separate but equal" ruling.

But the effort to bring these cases and argue them effectively became possible only after the NAACP was able to tap financial and other resources that had not been available in the African-American community in the past. The great migrations of African-Americans to the North, especially in the years leading up to the second World War, brought about political changes that were not possible in the South because of disenfranchisement. African-Americans could, and did, vote in the North, especially in Northern cities such as Detroit, New York, Chicago and Philadelphia. They were often led by well-educated members of the African-American community who had learned how to use those votes to make alliances with local, political leaders. By doing so, they secured more jobs in local government and law enforcement, more effort to make trials fair, and greater access, in general, to the privileges that local, European-Americans enjoyed. During the Depression, African-Americans in the North became a key part of Roosevelt's coalition. While that coalition included segregationist Democrats from the South, and hence would not make any radical changes in social practices, the New Deal policies and programs helped many African-American communities immensely. The increase in demand for labor, due to the second World War, helped put African-Americans in better paying jobs. Many became part of unions. They also served admirably in World War II, though the military was still segregated and African-American soldiers were continually faced with bigotry. The fame of units such as the 332nd fighter group, the Tuskegee Airman, who never lost a bomber to enemy fire, began to spread. How could their intelligence or bravery be regarded as inferior when the technical expertise of mechanics, pilots and others, as well as their courage, was so exemplary?

Brown v. Board of Education (1954)

New appointees to the Supreme Court, during these years, had lived in a world in which African-American participation in politics, the economy and the war effort had become more and more apparent and acceptable. The desegregation of the military which began in 1948, and the integration of professional baseball which began with Jackie Robinson in 1947, both heralded a comfort, more so in the North, with Americans of African and European decent living together in society. The political ideology of the war itself, which contrasted American democracy and freedom to Nazi fascism, also influenced views about segregation. Wartime propaganda argued against the Master Race ideology of the Nazi party, but, by extension, also undercut segregationist views about differences between African-Americans and European Americans. Nevertheless, the newfound comfort in racial relations could always change, as leaders in the African-American community knew from the past. They would need to tap into the resources of their community to wage a battle of more lasting effect on advancing the rights of African-Americans.

Justice Harlan's dissent in *Plessy* was the basis of the Supreme Court's opinion in *Brown v. Board, of Education* (1954), which declared segregation in pubic schools contrary to, and in violation of, the Fourteenth Amendment. Pursuant to the Court's ruling it is now unconstitutional to separate children from one another in public schools on the basis of their race. Charles Hamilton Houston, James Nabrit, and Thurgood Marshall engineered the legal strategy for overcoming segregation in the courts. They started at the graduate level, concluding that it would be more costly for the state to provide separate but equal facilities for adults. For example, almost twenty years before *Brown*, in *Missouri ex rel. Gaines v. Canada*,[10] Houston argued that the state of Missouri denied African-American students an equal legal education.[11] The University of Missouri
School of Law did not admit African-American students, who had to study law in a bordering state that accepted them. The Court said that this system was unconstitutional, and that if separate accommodations were not available, then the African-American student could go to the white school.[12]

---

[10]   305 U.S. 337 (1938)
[11]   *See also Sweatt v. Painter*, 339 U.S. 629 (1950) and *McClaurin v. Oklahoma State Regents*, 339 U.S. 637 (1950).
[12]   *Missouri ex rel. Gaines v. Canada*, 305 U.S. 337 (1938)

As noted, the case of *Missouri ex rel Gaines v. Canada* was a beginning in the quest of the NAACP law team to use the Constitution to dismantle the Jim Crow laws in the South, and segregation anywhere in the country. The NAACP held planning conferences for lawyers working on desegregating schools. They used financial resources of the organization, which had grown rapidly, to work with experts from academia and argue against the pseudo-scientific views about differences between African-Americans and European-Americans.

The court cases themselves slowed during the war years. Then, in 1948, they won the *Shelley v. Kraemer* case which asserted that neighborhood covenants, restricting neighborhoods by race, were unconstitutional whenever they were enforced by a state. That year, they also won the *Sipuel v. Board of Regents* case. While the case resembled the Gaines case of 1938, the effect was different in that the losing side (Oklahoma University) decided to admit African-American students to classes with European-Americans, for courses that were not provided for them separately by the school. In other words, by enforcing "separate but equal" and insisting that it had to be truly "equal," the NAACP put an economic burden on those who wanted continue with segregation. Indeed, this was part of the plan. As segregation became more expensive, they hoped it would be enforced less. Two more decisions, in 1950, *Sweatt v. Painter* and *McLaurin v. Oklahoma Regents*, made it much more difficult to provide African-Americans with anything short of what was equal, if they were to live, work or learn separately from European-Americans.

But, while these decisions helped improve some conditions and increase opportunity, they also reinforced "separate but equal" as a doctrine. Indeed, many school districts, especially in the South, began plans to build separate schools for African-Americans, or renovate existing ones, to comply with the ruling. Some NAACP leaders thought that it might be best to comply with such a program, as long as there were some smaller scale efforts at desegregation. It would create equal facilities, equal resources. It would constitute a plateau on the long struggle upwards. But when other school districts staunchly opposed such "equalizing" efforts, the organization, after a national strategy meeting in 1950, made plans to push for universal desegregation by overturning Plessy.

The NAACP carefully chose five cases to bring forward. They argued that the schools for African-Americans, in these communities, were inferior to those for European-Americans. But they argued, further, that the policy of "separate but equal" was itself unconstitutional, with regard to the Fourteenth Amendment. School segregation on the basis of ethnicity was, regardless of material conditions and resources, inherently unequal. During some of these cases, the NAACP lawyers developed the strategy of bringing in academic experts, social scientists for the most part, to back up these claims of inherent inequality with regard to the effect on African-American children. While the cases were lost for one reason or another, the Supreme Court agreed to review all five cases in 1952. Once again, social scientists were brought in to give evidence that segregation in the schools was inherently unequal. In 1953, when the Court ruled that the case should be reargued, and asked a number of historical questions aimed at defining the intent of those who had framed the Fourteenth Amendment, academic experts were brought in once again. While such testimony was proving to be more and more effective, it was also expensive, and the NAACP had to raise more and more money.

After working and re-working the evidence, lawyers filed a brief for the case of *Brown v. Board of Education of the City of Topeka*. Historical analysis of documents strongly suggested that the intent of the Fourteenth Amendment had been to outlaw segregation generally, and specifically in public schools. Legislators who were uncomfortable with the basis for the Civil Rights Law of 1866 had looked to the Fourteenth Amendment to validate Congressional power to combat state segregation practices. The "separate but equal" doctrine in *Plessy* ran counter to this intent, and was an error. The brief further argued that efforts to remedy segregation in schools could not be put off, but needed to be addressed quite soon. In 1954, the Supreme Court handed the NAACP its greatest victory when it unanimously agreed that state segregation of schools on the basis of race was unconstitutional, that the *Plessy* ruling of "separate but equal" was no longer valid, and that school districts should make a clear and continuing effort to desegregate schools.

Bibliography

John A. Garraty, editor. *Quarrels That Have Shaped The Constitution*, revised and expanded edition. New York: Harper & Row Publishers, Inc., 1987

Vincent Harding. *There Is A River: The Black Struggle for Freedom in America.* New York: Vintage Books, 1983.

George Brown Tindall. *America: A Narrative History*, vols. 1 and 2, 2nd ed. New York: W.W. Norton & Company, 1988.

Appendix II:
Events, Institutions and Movements Shaping Post-Brown v. Board of Education

Subchapters:

The Murder of Emmett Till (August 1955)

The Montgomery Bus Boycott (December 1955-December 1956)

Civil Rights Groups of the South
    Lynching and the founding of the NAACP
    W.E.B. DuBois and the Niagara Movement
    Opposition to the NAACP
    Southern Christian Leadership Conference (SCLC)
    Student Nonviolent Coordinating Committee (SNCC)
    Medgar Evers

Putting *Brown v. Board* into Practice
    Little Rock Desegregation (1957-1958)
    The Lost Year (1958-1959)
    Desegregation elsewhere

Greensboro and the Lunch Counter Sit-Ins
    Congress Of Racial Equality (CORE) and previous Sit-Ins (1942, 1949, 1952)
    Student-led Greensboro Sit-In (1960)
    Other Sit-Ins, Swim-Ins, Pray-Ins (1960+)
    Student Nonviolent Coordinating Committee (SNCC)

Freedom Rides
    1947 CORE and the Journey of Reconciliation
    1961 Freedom Ride

Patriotism, Racism and the Red Scare
    Cold War Politics and the Labor Movement
    Jewish and Latin-American Civil Rights Efforts
    Realistic Patriotism vs. Complacent Patriotism

The Black Church
    Historical role of religion in black America
    Social Gospel Movement
    Black Preachers

The Murder of Emmett Till (August 1955)

There were many instances of grotesque violence committed against African-Americans in the history of America: some will remain unknown, others will be remembered by a few, and still others will stand out in the conscience of the nation. The brutal murder of a 14 year-old, young man from Chicago, Emmett Till, stands in this latter category. The brutality itself, of course, is infamous enough, but the story of how it happened and the consequences for those who committed such brutality, along with the timing, all help establish it as a sad and bitter memory in our nation's history that must not be forgotten.

Emmett was murdered, by some accounts, because he startled a European-American lady while on a visit with relatives in Mississippi. Years later, as various accounts of the actions were pieced together, we understand some of the events, and perhaps some of the reasons for an atrocity so unreasonable.

Emmett, who was from Chicago, was visiting Money, Mississippi with a cousin, Wheeler Parker, to see other cousins and his great-uncle Mose Wright. One Wednesday, August 24th, he and other youngsters had worked picking cotton and then had gone into town to relax, eat some sweets and have fun. While in Bryant's Grocery and Meat Market, a store where African-Americans often shopped, he said, or did something that offended Carolyn Bryant, wife of Roy Bryant, the store's owners, who was working that day because Roy was away. She reacted by leaving immediately, scaring the youngsters who thought she was going to get a pistol from her car. They fled in a car.

In court, after the murder, Carolyn Bryant testified that Emmett had put his arm around her waist and said lewd things; some accounts say he had asked her for a date. According to one witness, Emmett had put his money in her hand, not on the counter as was expected in the race-conscious, etiquette of the South. Emmett had a stutter, the result of suffering from Polio when he was young, and some think that his speech may have confused Bryant and led to a misunderstanding. When she was outside the store, some witnesses said Emmett had whistled at her. From many accounts, he liked to joke around.

From what we can tell, Carolyn Bryant did not tell her husband about the encounter, but enough people saw one or another aspect of the encounter that word got around and Roy eventually found out. After he, and his half brother, J.W. Milam kidnapped Emmett two days later from Mose Wright's cabin, murdered him in brutal fashion and were acquitted of all charges, they sold their story to Look Magazine for 4000 dollars. In the article, they admitted killing Emmett, but said that, initially, they had only meant to 'teach him a lesson.'

The reasons will, perhaps, remain forever unclear. If a young person acts in a way that surprises or even offends an adult, the adult could just explain the offense and ask for an apology and a commitment to behave differently in the future. But in this case, as in others involving African-Americans in the segregated South, unfounded assumptions that African-Americans did not have the same educational and moral capabilities as European-Americans led some to habitually treat the former as they might treat a wild animal that needed to be broken and tamed: not with admonitions and explanations, but with threats and swift brutality.

Roy Bryant talked like he expected Emmett Till to behave differently after the beating, to act more subservient perhaps. In statements made after the jury found him innocent, Bryant said that his original intention was to 'teach' the young man a lesson. If that really was his intent, he seems to suggest that Till did not take to the 'lesson' in the way Bryant wanted. Whether he was courageously defiant, or just resolved that he was about to die, it may be that Till did not act as the Bryant wanted, and that that led to more anger and brutality, to disfiguring the boy, poking out an eye so it hung from his face, bashing in his nose and finally killing him with a gun, tying his head to a cotton gin fan with barbed wire, and dumping his body into the Tallahatchie river. Or it may be that the brutality was intended from the beginning. We only have Bryant's words about his original intent; Till's intentions were obscured before the trial even began.

In the end, this young man's body was so horribly disfigured that it was only dental records that could identify him. His mother had to fight to gain access to his body and have it taken up North for burial; gaining the legal means to do so just before it was to be buried in Mississippi without ceremony or any relatives around. She had to fight Southern officials to have the casket opened for public viewing at the funeral, again gaining legal means to have padlocks and the seal of the State of Mississippi removed. The people responsible for this atrocity had been found innocent by a jury of their peers, in less than an hour, and had then admitted to the crime afterwards. What justice could be garnered in these circumstances was the justice of raw facts; the world would see how hideously those men had brutalized and disfigured her son. The jury could, it seems, argue away the crime as a necessary part of life for a European-American in the South, but perhaps the disgusting details would defy that kind of judgment in the minds of others.

Emmett Till's brutal murder, the trial (however unsuccessful) and the media coverage caught the attention of a nation that, for so long, had been content to 'look the other way' with regard to the Jim Crow South. There are some things that are local concerns: fines for parking tickets, speed limits on local roads; but something in the conscience of people around America was stirred by the details of this atrocity, by a system of oppression that, to many, now seemed more of a universal concern than a local one. Something was stirred in the conscience of African-Americans in the South as well. At the trial, for the first time that anyone could remember in Mississippi, an African-American man, Emmett's great-uncle Mose Wright, had testified against European-American men, and lived. Nor was he the last African-American to stand up to segregation, as the nation found out several months later.

The Montgomery Bus Boycott (December 1, 1955—December 20, 1956)

Jo Ann Robinson, a professor at Alabama State College and the president of the Women's Political Council (WPC), had been advocating for a bus boycott in Montgomery since she had experienced harsh treatment on a bus back in 1949, but could not get enough support from her own colleagues in the WPC. To some, segregation on the buses was, regrettably, just another feature of the landscape in Alabama. When she was contacted by E.D. Nixon the evening of December 1st, 1955, professor Robinson realized that this was her best opportunity to galvanize the support of her colleagues and the rest of the African-American community in Montgomery. He had just bailed Rosa Parks out of jail and convinced her to use her case to test local segregation laws in the courts. Nixon had worked for years, as a leader of the state chapter of the Brotherhood of Sleeping Car Porters and the state and local chapters of the National Association for the Advancement of Colored People (NAACP), to organize African-Americans against political and economic oppression. While he phoned local, African-American community leaders (including Rev. Martin Luther King, Jr.) to ask for their support, professor Robinson, with the help of a colleague and two students, mimeographed 35,000 fliers calling for a one-day, bus boycott. Interestingly, professor Robinson did not wait for the group of ministers and other community leaders Nixon was calling to meet and discuss the boycott. Nor did she wait for Rosa Park's views on the matter. It seems that professor Robinson wanted to push matters along out of concern that more conservative leaders in the African-American community might try to stall or oppose the boycott. They worked until 4AM the next morning, setting the date of the boycott for Monday, December 5th. Like the efforts she had made with other African-American women in the WPC, the boycott was aimed at drawing attention to the unfairness and indecency of segregation by flexing the economic muscle of the African-American community.

A number of other, African-American women had defied the segregation policies on city buses in Montgomery, and been arrested for their defiance. African-American community leaders had considered supporting many of them to challenge the segregation laws, but they believed that they needed a person whose conduct and personal history would not prove to be a distraction from the effort to discredit and overturn segregation laws. For instance, they considered supporting Claudette Colvin, a fifteen-year old, African-American young lady who had refused to give up her seat on a bus to a European-American person, but changed their minds when they learned that she was pregnant with the child of a married man. Her case had merit, and would eventually become part of a federal case against segregation more generally, but her individual circumstances would, it was believed, distract community members from the case itself and drain support from the effort. But Rosa Parks, who had worked as a secretary for the local NAACP and who was respected in the community, seemed a much better choice.

Rosa Parks had not planned on sparking a year-long, bus boycott. Like most African-Americans in the Montgomery area, she had learned to put up with the unfairness and humiliation that segregation policies cultivated. As a youngster, she walked to school with other African-American children while watching the European-American children take school buses to the white-only schools in town. She had learned that the 'white' and 'black' sections of buses could change, depending on how many European-Americans were in the bus, so that African-Americans often had to change seats as the 'white' section expanded. She had experienced the humiliation of having to use the front door of the bus to pay her fare, but then having to exit and use the back door to enter again and find her seat. On a rainy day in 1943, she had taken a seat in the 'white' section, momentarily, when her purse had dropped on the way out the front door. The driver, James Blake, was so angry that as soon as she stepped out the front door, he drove away, before she could reenter the bus by the back door. She had to walk home five miles in the rain that day.

While she did not plan out her defiance of the bus seating policy, Mrs. Parks had a number of experiences that may have helped motivate her for what she did. She worked for a time at Maxwell Air Force Base, where the trolleys were not segregated. She attended workshops, in 1954 and the summer of 1955, at the *Highlander Folk School* in Monteagle, TN, where civil rights leaders (including Dr. King) and labor leaders had met to discuss how best to deal with economic and racial problems. Looking back, she recalled: "I noticed [at Highlander in 1954] how Septima Clark could organize and hold things together in this very informal setting of interracial living. I had to admire this great woman. I was just the opposite. I was tense, and I was nervous, and I was upset most of the time….I felt that I had been destroyed long ago." (Rosa Parks quoted in Everybody Says Freedom, 25) Four days before her protest began she had heard presentations at church about the fairly recent murder of several Africa-Americans, including Emmett Till. All of these experiences helped cultivate the steely determination on Thursday, December 1st, 1955, not to move back when the bus driver, James Blake again, enlarged the 'white' section and ordered Rosa and three other African-American passengers to move. She was the steel, and the plans and decades of work of Nixon, Robinson and others were the flint that, together, ignited a protest and inaugurated a movement.

As someone respected in both the European-American community, as well as the African-American community, Rose Parks was the perfect catalyst for a grand, nonviolent protest of segregation on city buses, but initially this was only a one-day protest to support Mrs. Parks on the day she went to court. As mentioned, professor Robinson worked all night with a colleague and two students so that the fliers calling for the boycott could be distributed around the community on Friday, before the weekend. With the help of Rev. Ralph Abernathy and others, she distributed fliers at local high schools. Bundles of fliers were dropped off at other locations. They wanted the local churches to be able to discuss the matter and generate support on Sunday, as well.

That Friday, Nixon had managed to bring together about fifty leaders of the African-American community in Montgomery for a meeting at Dexter Avenue Baptist Church where the Rev. Martin Luther King Jr. had only recently accepted the pastorship. The group, which later took the name the Montgomery Improvement Association (MIA), decided to hold a meeting on Monday night, after the boycott, for the entire African-American community, at Holt Street Baptist Church. The purpose would be to decide if the boycott should be continued.

The one-day boycott met with great success; buses ran virtually empty and at the meeting that evening the community agreed to extend the boycott. Their main demand was that the dividing line between 'white' and 'black' sections of the buses be made permanent, so that if the 'white' section were filled, additional European-American passengers would have to stand and African-American passengers could not be asked to move further back. They also asked for the drivers to treat all passengers with courtesy and asked for the bus company to begin hiring African-American drivers. These were modest demands, but significant.

Indeed, they mirrored the demands of other one-day boycotts that had been organized in other parts of the South. As it happened, Rev. King had invited an activist, T.R.M. Howard of the Regional Council of Negro Leadership, from Mississippi, to speak at his church in several days before Rosa Parks' arrest, on a similar boycott, several years earlier, that had been organized by to oppose gas stations that did not have facilities for African-Americans. Indeed, there had been several one-day boycotts over bus segregation in the past few years, e.g., one in Baton Rouge, Louisiana in 1953. These demands, like others, fell short of demanding full desegregation on buses, but offered a more polite, respectful and equal 'separateness' on bus transportation. Despite this effort at compromise, city officials led by Mayor W.A. Gayle refused to budge.

Rev. King had recently finished all but his dissertation at Boston University, and every since he'd begun preaching at Dexter, he was eager for a more socially engaged congregation. One of the new committees he set up, the social and political action committee was charged forging close ties with, and appreciation for, the NAACP. He also wanted every member of the congregation to register to vote. Rev. King had begun to forge ties to other groups in the area, such as the interracial Alabama Council on Human Relations, and had impressed NAACP members at a chapter meeting in August of 1955, so much so that he received a letter from the chapter secretary, Rosa Parks, naming him to the chapter's executive committee soon afterward, and with three months of that, he was asked to serve as president of the chapter (though he declined the latter, citing his work and his wife's pregnancy). So he was not unknown, despite his short time in town, and with the support of Nixon and several others, the MIA members were persuaded to choose Rev. King to serve as president of the MIA. Nixon himself was eager for a strong leader who had not yet been intimidated by leaders in the European-American community. The fact that Rev. King was new to the Montgomery community was also helpful in that he had not yet settled into any of the cliques within the local African-American community, and would be seen as less divisive than other attendees.

The MIA faced many difficulties as the boycott continued. People still needed to go to work, and the logistics of helping them do so while avoiding the buses became more and more challenging. Initially, African-American taxis lowered their rates to ten cents from forty-five, in support of the boycott. But this only worked until city officials threatened to fine any driver who used rates at the level that the bus company had been granted. Some people could walk or ride bikes; others were given rides from friends with a car, or from European-Americans who had employed them in their homes and businesses and didn't want the boycott to stop them from working.

City officials and organizations, with the help of members the White Citizens' Council and the Ku Klux Klan, used legal as well as physical means to break the will of the MIA and the Africa-American boycott of the city buses. For instance, city leaders tried to sow seeds of discontent within the MIA by suggesting that Rev. King was a young, outsider who had taken control of MIA from older members of the community. Emotions flared at one MIA meeting and Rev. King offered to step down, but the board moved to give him full support.

As the boycott continued, MIA leaders get threatening phone calls, esp. Rev. King. Others, including Rev. Abernathy, the European-American Rev. Graetz and E.D. Nixon had property vandalized and bombed. European-American city leaders charged that the boycott was being pushed on local African-Americans from outside forces, "good squads" as they called them. City officials also used their influence to get the insurance on cars used in the MIA carpool rescinded, crippling the carpool until MIA officials were able to secure outside car insurance.

On Saturday, January 21st, city officials, with active help of local paper, tricked three African-American ministers who were not working with the MIA to end the boycott without any basic change in the bus policy. They hoped to trick the majority of African-Americans to start using the buses again before the MIA could do anything about it. But the MIA leaders acted quickly after an African-American reporter, Carl T. Rowan, from Minneapolis, who had visited Montgomery and the MIA a few weeks before, picked up the story from the wire service and failed to recognize the names of the three ministers. He contacted Reverend King, who wasn't aware of any settlement. MIA people passed the word around popular places of entertainment that night. Rev. King and other MIA leaders worked the phones Saturday night so that African-American ministers in town would tell their congregations the next day that, regardless of what the newspapers said, the boycott was still on.

With the trick failing, Mayor Gayle called off any further negotiations and announced a "get tough" policy, the hallmark of which would be police harassment. Since the voluntary carpool system was helping African-Americans get to work and around town, police followed the cars in the carpool and arrested them for minor infractions or for nothing at all. Rev. King himself, when he gave three people a ride from one of the MIA carpool locations, was followed by police and thrown in jail until bond could be arranged. Rev. Abernathy raised the cash necessary to keep Rev. King from a night in jail.

On Monday, January 30th, while Rev. King and others were at the night mass meeting, a bomb was exploded on his porch. Mrs. King and a friend had heard a noise and footsteps and had retreated into the back of the home, and were not hurt, but of course this was the very thing Rev. King had feared that night. When informed, however, he calmly told the people present, left, and went home. When a crowd gathered and the mayor and police commissioner worried about violence, Rev. King was able to reassure the crowd and urge them to keep calm. They stayed at the house of a friend, but again that night, they heard a noise; this time someone was knocking. Later, the phone rang; it was Rev. King's father, Daddy King who had driven all the way from Atlanta along with Rev. King Jr.'s brother and sister. Soon they were joined by Mrs. King's father. Both were urging the King's to leave Montgomery and go back to Atlanta, but neither would leave.

Over the next month, pressure to leave Montgomery from Rev. King's family and friends in Atlanta became intense, but both resisted. After a mass encounter of friends and family in Atlanta, Rev. King argued so forcefully that he had to stay in Montgomery and continue with the boycott and the MIA that the consensus formed to respect his decision. People present, however, contacted NAACP legal officials, including chief counsel Thurgood Marshall, to get assurances that Rev. King would get the best legal help they could provide, as the boycott continued.

In response to intimidation by members of the European-American community, MIA leaders took several steps. They increased the number of mass meetings from two to six. They also considered and eventually applied for legal status to taxi people around town and charge a small fee. They were denied on several grounds.

On a more personal level, Rev. King contemplateed stepping down. On Friday, January 27th, several more threatening phone calls lead to his crisis at midnight. He couldn't sleep and went to make coffee, but his thoughts went to his newborn daughter, smiling gently in sleep, and his wife. He could lose them; they could lose him. But there were no answers. His father, to whom he could always turn for help, was far away in Atlanta. He felt alone, so he prayed. He admitted his uncertainty, his fear, his lack of resolve. His mind told him that their cause was right and just, but he could not commit to it fully when faced with so many pressures. In answer, he heard a voice reassuring him , telling him to stand up for justice and God would be with him always. Soon after, a new strength grew inside him. He was no longer uncertain; he could weather the storm of his campaign.

The bombing emboldened the MIA to change tactics and oppose segregation on the buses directly. When a group of businessmen, the Men of Montgomery, worked to avoid the mass indictments that city officials were preparing, based on an anti-boycotting law, and secured most of the original demands, the MIA presented the offer at a mass meeting and it was rejected. They would not compromise now; they would press for full integration.

The MIA responded to a variety of other troubles. Rev. King and Rev. Abernathy did not believe the police would protect them or their families as well as they'd promised after the bombing, so they applied for pistol permits, which were not immediately granted. While preaching at a church in Chicago, King met with officials in the United Packinghouse Workers union to consider union pressure on the Chicago headquarters for the City Lines bus company that operated in Montgomery.

When mass indictments of MIA people were finally issued, the MIA turned the occasion into a celebration of sorts, dressing in their best clothes to be arrested, while a crowd of five thousand sang hymns. They got the attention of national papers, such as the New York Times, as well as television news. It also got the attention of activists such as Bayard Rustin and A. Philip Randolph, both of whom thought that the MIA's efforts could, perhaps, be expanded with outside help to fight segregation throughout the South. Rustin traveled to Montgomery to learn more, but did not stay long. Local MIA people were not comfortable with outside organizations getting involved, and people in the New York pacifist groups who knew Rustin warned him that his one-time membership in the Young Communist League, along with the fact that he was homosexual, would almost certainly distract the MIA's efforts if local officials learned about them.

The efforts also drew the attention of members of the Fellowship of Reconciliation (FOR). The Fellowship was an international, mostly European and American group that first met to try to prevent the first World War, and continued to fight nonviolently for peace and justice. They fought for civil liberties, helped Jews escape the Nazi's, fought against the internment of Japanese-Americans during the second World War. They also worked with the Labor movement in the 30s to secure better working conditions and sponsored the first, but little known, "freedom ride" called the "Journey of Reconciliation" in 1947 (Rustin had participated in it.). Rev. Glenn Smiley of FOR met with Dr. King in Montgomery and realized that without much knowledge of Gandhi, Rev. King was embodying many principles of nonviolent resistance that paralleled those of Gandhi. They talked about nonviolence, and Smiley gave Rev. King several books on nonviolence, which King accepted. He seemed eager to learn more about Gandhi's ideas. Smiley later contacted friends and colleagues, describing Rev. King as, potentially, a "Negro Gandhi." His reports to friends and associates, such as James Farmer, Philip Randolph and others prompted them to try to garner national support for the MIA's activities, but also won their respect, since the MIA, without knowledge of nonviolent techniques, had put into practice their own, quite nonviolent campaign against segregation.

Things moved very slowly on the legal front at first. Because they weren't asking for full desegregation, the NAACP (already supported cases for full desegregation for buses in

Columbia, South Carolina) did not feel it should participate in Montgomery protests. Indeed, the Montgomery paper, the Advertiser, noted that several Southern cities: Mobile, Huntsville, Nashville and Macon, already had bus segregation policies which mirrored the MIA's plan. Initially, the MIA stated they were keeping in line with "separate, but equal" of Plessy v. Ferguson decision of 1896. By the end of January, legal advisors had convinced MIA leaders that the Rosa Parks case, while a lightning rod for community support, would have to be appealed through the Alabama State Court system, and could be slowed down for quite some time by various procedures. They began to file papers for a federal case, involving a number of women who had been arrested for violating the segregation policy.

Eventually, after NAACP mass meetings elsewhere had garnered funds, and with the spur of Rev. King, the NAACP began to contribute funds for the MIA members, legal defense, for the federal case, and for Mrs. Parks defense. The boycott held for over a year, with people walking, riding backs, taking horse-drawn carriages, as well as using black taxi's and the MIA carpool and other transit plans. There were collections to supply shoes for people who were wearing out their current pairs. In November of 1956, the Supreme Court upheld a federal court decision that the bussing segregation laws violated the Brown v. Board decision and that they were unconstitutional. Finally, on December 20th, once the city passed a new ordinance, effectively ending segregation on city buses, the boycott ended, and a Civil Rights Movement was born.

In a country that prides itself on free enterprise and the free choice of consumers to spend their money as they will, opposition to the Montgomery Bus Boycott was profoundly ironic. What could be more 'American' than people freely choosing which services to use and which to forgo? Nevertheless, when African-Americans organized to boycott city buses they were criticized, intimidated and harassed. But in addition to being ironic, the Montgomery Bus Boycott was one of the first grand examples of nonviolent opposition to injustice in Post-*Brown v. Board* America.

Civil Rights Groups and the South

There were several more prominent civil rights groups active in the South after *Brown v. Board of Education* came down, along with numerous, smaller groups. The National Association for the Advancement of Colored People (NAACP) was the oldest and best established civil rights organization, but the movement gained new tactics and energy when the Southern Christian Leadership Conference (SCLC) was formed shortly after the Montgomery Bus Boycott, and again when the Student Nonviolent Coordinating Committee (SNCC) was formed shortly after the Greensboro Sit-Ins began. These groups were distinct, though they sometimes worked together and/or aided one another, though there were some important differences between them.

Riots, Lynchings, and the National Association for the Advancement of Colored People (NAACP)

The race riots in Springfield, Illinois in 1908 shocked many who thought the country had made progress in race relations since the Civil War had ended. Not only was Illinois considered a northern state, but Springfield was the location of Abraham Lincoln's home. Two African-American men had been jailed for murder and sexual assault against European-Americans, but a crowd of European-Americans discovered which jail they were at and gathered to dish out their version of justice. Police secretly moved the two men to a jail sixty miles away, and when the crowd learned that they had been fooled, they became angry and began to riot, destroying scores of buildings and other property and attacking African-Americans, killing seven.

Mary White Ovington, a journalist who had worked for women's rights and various causes became even more committed to helping African-Americans after hearing Frederick Douglass speak in 1890. She worked and lived in New York City, studying and documenting working and living conditions for African-Americans. After reading an account of the Springfield Race Riots in 1908, by William Walling, she contacted him and the two met sometime later in New York with Dr. Henry Moskowitz to lay plans for a conference and an organization dedicated to securing the rights of African-Americans. With the support of early members, such as Josephine Ruffin, Mary Talbert, Inez Milholland, Oswald Garrison Villard, Charles Darrow, John Dewey, Jane Addams and Ida Wells-Barnett, to name a few, they established an organization first called the National Negro Committee in 1909 and then the National Association for the Advancement of Colored People (NAACP) in 1910. They aimed to work against the disenfranchisement of African-American voting rights that was in full swing in Southern states, as well as fight against other injustices and crimes, such as discrimination, the 'separate, but equal' polities, rioting and lynching. The early NAACP gained additional vigor when it merged with many of the members of the Niagara Movement, most prominently, W.E.B. DuBois.

W.E.B. DuBois and the Niagara Movement

The Niagara Movement was an organization of Africa-Americans started in 1905 with the aim of setting out a more robust and outspoken protest to combat the injustices, hardships and crimes that were being suffered by the African-American community. Following the lead of

W.E.B. DuBois, the group aimed to distinguish themselves from the more quiet and accommodating approach to addressing injustice and economic hardship which had been advanced by Booker T. Washington. They met at Niagara Falls in 1905 and in Harper's Ferry, West Virginia in 1906. They brought some cases forward, but did not have a lot of financial resources. When it was clear that their goals dovetailed with those of the NAACP many members merged with the NAACP, with DuBois taking on a prominent role in the later organization, especially with the publication of *The Crisis*.

Legal Campaign for Social and Economic Justice
In addition to working for anti-lynching legislation, the NAACP directed energies to publicizing injustices and atrocities as well as mounting a highly organized, and eventually well-financed legal challenge to various aspects of the unjust, Jim Crow system of segregation. The legal plans of Charles Hamilton Houston established a path to ending segregation by taking carefully chosen cases up to the Supreme Court. Victory in these cases needed the help of experts from academia, to assure judges of the effects of segregation on people, young and old, and organizing these experts took time and financial resources. The NAACP moved on many fronts, advancing legal challenges with a team of lawyers led by Thurgood Marshall, and tapping into the financial resources of middle-class, African-American businessmen to sustain the entire effort. Their efforts reached an important and transformational plateau in 1954 with the *Brown v. Board of Education* decision which effectively declared segregation and the 'separate, but equal' policy unconstitutional.

The Congress for Racial Equality (CORE) and Fellowship for Reconciliation (FOR)
This organization was begun by an interracial group of students at the University of Chicago in 1942, and was able to spread its influence and teachings throughout the country, helping to bring nonviolent methods to the growing struggle against injustice with regard to civil rights. CORE was an outgrowth of the Fellowship of Reconciliation (FOR), an interfaith organization dedicated to world peace, justice and nonviolence which was founded in 1914 after an ecumenical conference in Switzerland which tried, and failed, to prevent the first World War. Two of the participants, an English Quaker and a German Lutheran, met in the train station after the conference and pledged to work together for peace, despite their countries being at war. Less than a year later, FOR was established in England and the branch in the United States was founded the following year. Over the years, FOR worked to set up the forerunner to the American Civil Liberties Union (ACLU), helped work toward better living conditions for workers during the Labor Movement, helped Jews and member of other groups escape the atrocities of the Nazis, worked against the internment of Japanese-Americans during WWII, and held workshops on nonviolence for various groups during the Civil Rights Movement. James Farmer, a student at the University of Chicago and the race-relations director of FOR served as the first National Director of CORE in 1942.

Opposition to the NAACP (Alabama, 1956-1964)
It should be no surprise that state governments, especially in the South, which had administered a system of segregation for three-quarters of a century would find creative ways to resist the call for integration, and that some of these efforts would be directed at civil rights organizations such as the NAACP. Between 1956 and 1964, the NAACP was effectively barred from operating in the state of Alabama. The charges against the NAACP noted several offenses, including aiding the Montgomery Bus Boycott, and the effort to test the state's segregation laws. Not only had the NAACP provided legal help for Rosa Parks, but it had done so for two students who had attempted to enroll at the University of Alabama Law School and been denied. Nevertheless, the technical issue at the nub of the 1956 court order against the NAACP had also focused on the refusal of the NAACP, an organization based outside the state, to provide officials with a list of names and addresses of its members in Alabama. Other organizations had not been asked to do this, and it was assumed that the reason the NAACP was being asked was to make it easier for opponents of the NAACP to harass members and their families.

The appeals moved back and forth in State courts, and eventually in federal court, until finally, in 1964, the original ruling barring them from operating in Alabama was reversed by the Supreme Court. The effect, however, was that the NAACP had been blocked from participating fully, or at all, in various activities in the state for eight years of the civil rights movement. In response to the ruling against the NAACP, the Reverend Fred Shuttlesworth worked with others in 1956 to bring together a new organization, one that was more local than the NAACP, concentrated in Alabama: the Alabama Christian Movement for Human Rights (ACMHR). The group held demonstrations and boycotts to protest segregation in schools and at lunch counters. They were effective enough that Rev. Shuttlesworth's home was bombed late in 1956, and he, himself, was visciously beaten in 1957 when he tried to enroll his children in a local, all-white school. It was in 1957 that Rev. Shuttlesworth and others in ACMHR worked with Dr. King to form the Southern Christian Leadership Conference

Southern Christian Leadership Conference (SCLC)
This organization was formed in 1957 in the wake of the successful Montgomery Bus Boycott, as other groups across the South began bus boycotts of their own. In January of 1957, members of the Montgomery Improvement Association (MIA) met with representatives of other groups with the hope of working together in a larger civil rights organization for the South. At the January meeting in Atlanta, they took the name, the Southern Leadership Conference on Transportation and Nonviolent Integration, but a month later at another meeting in New Orleans the name became Southern Leadership Conference, which was finally changed to the Southern Christian Leadership Conference (SCLC) at a third conference later that year in Atlanta.

The aim was to apply nonviolent methods of protest to large numbers of people in the hope of changing not just the customs of segregation, but the attitudes and ideas which fostered those customs. The larger goals of SCLC paralleled those of the NAACP, in that they wanted to help improve the economic, social and political realities of African-Americans generally, but the membership and leadership of SCLC came from the Black Church. Voter registration was a part of their efforts, but so was the kind of mass action that would not only attract attention to problems and injustices that the European-American community would have rather overlooked, but also reach out to members of the European-American community to encourage them to question their usual ways of thinking and behaving. SCLC planned and took part in boycotts and marches, as well as voter registration drives. They also took over administration of the Citizenship School program that the Highlander Folk School had started. This program helped teach African-Americans to read and write, not only so that they could register to vote, but also so that they could fill out job applications and personal checks, among other things.

Because its membership was so much a part of the Black Church, SCLC would call on church-going African-Americans to participate in various activities, as well as keep in contact with the community through church meetings. This gave them resources with which other organizations were not as closely connected. The style of leadership in SCLC also duplicated the often top-down kind of authority that existed in black churches. Frequently, meetings to discuss mass actions would take place in church basements, and the singing of religious songs and freedom songs would be a large part of the meeting itself. The songs would help ease the fears of people who knew that their participation in such protests could affect their jobs, their lives, and the lives of their loved ones.

SCLC's activities aimed at fostering a beloved community in which people who were formerly enemies or strangers would become friends and neighbors. Their methods differed from the more legal and legislative approach of the NAACP, but they acted as another front in the battle against injustice; another way to carry on the struggle.

Student Nonviolent Coordinating Committee (SNCC)
In the wake of the sit-ins that began in Greensboro in early 1960, civil rights leaders saw the possibility of young people becoming more active in the movement. Ella Baker, the organizer who had worked in the NAACP and more recently in SCLC as the executive secretary lobbied for a conference of student leaders, at which they could meet, share stories, and discuss goals and tactics. She modeled it on the Highlander Folk School meeting for young activists, held in the early Spring, but wanted to get more people involved from a wider array of groups. The conference was held in April of 1960 at Shaw University in Raleigh, North Carolina and brought together about three hundred students. Baker had been critical of the top-down style of leadership at SCLC, and wanted the students to have a more grassroots, bottom-up approach to leadership.

During the conference, students decided that though they'd been supported by a grant from SCLC, they needed to set up their own group, the Student Nonviolent Coordinating Committee, which would plan and organize sit-ins and other nonviolent protest activities. So, in April of 1960, SNCC was born, with Marion Barry serving as its first chairman.

Students from several colleges in (e.g. Tennessee State University, The American Baptist Theological Seminary, Meherry Medical College, and Fisk University) Nashville, Tennessee, had been training in nonviolence since the Fall of 1959 under the direction of James Lawson, a divinity student at Vanderbilt University. Lawson had traveled to India as a Methodist missionary to study satyagraha, Gandhi's practice of nonviolent resistance to injustice, after having spent fourteen months in jail as a conscience objector to being drafted into the Korean War. After returning to the US in 1955 and briefly studying theology at Oberlin College in Ohio, Lawson had been persuaded by Dr. Martin Luther King Jr., to move to the South. In addition to studying theology at Vandy, Lawson served as the southern director for the Fellowship of Reconciliation (FOR) and organized a number of workshops on nonviolence. Student participants in these workshop and in the sit-ins in the Nashville area who later became members of SNCC included Diane Nash, John Lewis, James Bevel, Marion Barry and Bernard Lafayette. These students and their nonviolent training had a large impact on the early SNCC.

SNCC members led sit-ins, swim-ins (efforts to integrate segregated swimming pools), and pray-ins (efforts to integrate segregated churches), often being jailed for 'disorderly conduct' and/or attacked and beaten by counter-protesters who were tolerated by local law enforcement. They joined the Freedom Bus Ride of 1961 after the original members had been attacked, firebombed and hospitalized, in an effort to keep the protest against segregated bussing going in the face of state and local opposition and violence. SNCC also worked on voter registration and helped organize African-Americans politically, especially with the Freedom Ballot project in Mississippi in 1963. With the leadership of SNCC field secretary and co-director of the Council of Federated Organizations (COFO), Bob Moses, SNCC played a large role in the Freedom Summer Project in Mississippi and in the formation of the Mississippi Freedom Democratic Party. COFO worked with SNCC, SCLC, CORE and the NAACP to coordinate voter registration activities and distribute funds from the Voter Education Project (VEP), an effort of the Kennedy administration to bring money from several non-profit organizations to voter registration drives in the South, steering civil rights groups away from outright protest activity.

Protest continued, however, with the violence in Selma capturing the nation's and the world's attention. The Nashville influence on SNCC became displaced by the views of activists who became less than totally committed to nonviolence, and more willing to advocate violent, self-defense in the face of violence from white supremacy groups and groups of local people raised in a climate of prejudice and ignorance about racial and ethnic differences. SNCC became less active late in the 1960 and early 70s, as prominent members left to work with other groups.

Putting *Brown v. Board* into Practice
Little Rock Desegregation (1957-1958)

Roughly three years after the *Brown v. Board* of Education decision, in September of 1957, the desegregation of public schools began as nine, black high school students attempted to attend Central High in Little Rock, Arkansas.

Daisy Bates, president of Arkansas NAACP, and her husband L.C., who was the NAACP regional director and publisher of the state's biggest, black-owned newspaper, began the effort to get black students into the Little Rock white-only schools, after the *Brown v. Board* ruling came down in 1954, but the local officials were not eager to comply. The Bates' took the schools to court to force compliance, but they also began preparations for the actual students who would be the first to enter the school.

Mrs. Bates, who had no children of her own, loved children and knew many in the area. She also knew that finding the right students to inaugurate an integrated school district would be as important as it would be difficult. They would not only need to meet the approval of the school board officials, but they would need the support of their parents, who would know only too well just how dangerous this could become. They would all need the legal advice and support of the NAACP.

After word of the plan to have black students at Central High School in Little Rock got around town, pressure began to mount to stop integration. A group of women from a local church, who had questionable views about interracial dating, marriage and the spread of diseases, formally asked the Governor to stop the nine black students, who were preparing to attend school, from doing so. Governor Orval Faubus agreed to do so, despite Federal District Judge Ronald Davies' order to integrate the school.

The Governor gave the reason that he was stopping integration to prevent the violence which would surely follow it. He ordered Arkansas National Guard to prevent the students from attending, supposedly for their own safety. The students, led by Daisy Bates, tried to enter the school but were blocked by the Arkansas National Guard and an angry crowd of people. But the decision of a governor to defy a federal judge, and defy the U.S. Supreme Court by extension, raised the issues of federal vs. state powers, as well as the separation of powers, and the executive branch of the federal government, led by a former general, felt compelled to act.

By the end of the month, President Eisenhower had federalized the National Guard and sent in the 101st Airborne Division of the Army to protect the nine students and guarantee them access to Central High. The Bates, as well as the parents of the "Little Rock Nine," the black students who entered the school that year, were threatened throughout the year. Despite harassment by white students, the school was kept open for these black students that year and one of them, Ernest Green, graduated in the May of 1958.

The Lost Year (1958-1959)

Rather than allow black students access to the same school as white students, Governor Faubus closed the public schools in Little Rock for the entire school year of 1958-1959. That year has since been called the Lost Year. Teachers were paid to come to school and do nothing. All classes and school activities were canceled, except for the football program. Families who were determined to have their children attend school, especially families of seniors, found ways to hire teachers for their own private schools, or, if they did not have that kind of money, sent children to live with relatives in nearby towns where integration was not being initiated. For some without money or other towns to send their children, the school year was truly lost. Needless to say, it was a strange and difficult year. The schools were only reopened, a year later, when the closing was declared unconstitutional by the Supreme Court.

Greensboro and the Lunch Counter Sit-Ins
Congress Of Racial Equality (CORE) and previous Sit-Ins

A Sit-In is a form of nonviolent protest which aims to draw attention to unjust customs, actions and/or laws and persuade other people to work together to overturn these injustices. Like a boycott, a sit-in focuses on the economic reality of injustice. Instead of drawing attention and persuading others by withdrawing financial interactions from specific stores or service businesses at which one had previously spent money, however, the sit-in focus on areas of stores and more specific services which were unjustly and unreasonably forbidden for people of a particular group.

The first sit-in related to the struggle for civil rights was conducted by the newly formed Congress of Racial Equality (CORE) in 1943 in Chicago. Sit-ins were also held in St. Louis in 1949, Baltimore in 1953, Oklahoma in 1957 and Kansas in 1958, but each remained fairly isolated in effect. As mentioned, CORE, which was organized by an interracial group of students at the University of Chicago in 1942, was able to spread its influence and teachings throughout the country, helping to bring nonviolent methods to the growing struggle against injustice with regard to civil rights. CORE was an outgrowth of the Fellowship of Reconciliation (FOR), an interfaith organization dedicated to world peace, justice and nonviolence which was founded in 1914 after an ecumenical conference in Switzerland which tried, and failed, to prevent the first World War. James Farmer, a student at the University of Chicago and the race-relations director of FOR served as the first National Director of CORE in 1942.

Despite the work that CORE had done, the Sit-In movement of the 1960s was not generated from that group's members directly. Early in 1960, four freshmen, African-American students at North Carolina Agricultural and Technical College were talking one night about how they could help participate in the civil rights movement. They decided to have a sit-in the next day at the local Woolworth's store in Greensboro, NC. On February 1st, 1960, Joseph McNeil, Franklin McCain, David Richmond, and Ezell Blair Jr. entered the Woolworth's store, walked around and finally bought a few items: toothpaste, notebook paper, etc…. Having demonstrated that the store was willing to sell them these items, they then sat down at the "white-only" counter to buy hotdogs and coffee, but they were ignored at first, and then refused. They remain seated though an African-American woman who was washing dishes there tells them to leave. A few older, European-American women pat them on the back and tell them their doing a good thing. A police officer enters, unhappy about the incident, but since the students are not acting violently, he does not do anything. Finally, the manager decides to close the store early and the four students leave.

The story makes it into the local student paper, and when the four return the next day, local European-American kids show up to harass them. Despite this, they remain nonviolent and continue their sit-in. The local media finds out and begins to cover the story. The next day, European-American women from North Carolina Women's College show up at Woolworth's as well, sitting down to eat but refusing to buy food until the African-American students are served. The media notes the contrast of jeering, swearing locals and the calm, respectful, sit-in protesters.

As the state and national media begin to report this over the next several days, similar sit-ins spring up in the North Carolina cities of Durham, Winston-Salem, Charlotte, Raleigh, Fayetteville and Elizabeth City, and throughout places in the South, such as Norfolk Virginia and Rock Hill, South Carolina. Younger people, primarily, spread the word, via telephone, to friends in other places. Within two weeks there are sit-ins in Nashville, Tennessee and Tallahassee, Florida.

The Nashville protests are organized with the help of Rev. James Lawson. Lawson had been to India to study Gandhi's nonviolent techniques. He had already been working with students on nonviolent protest methods in the Fall semester of 1959, but the stir of the growing sit-in movement moved him and his students into action. By February 18th, 200 students staged sit-ins against segregated dining at stores in Nashville. Most were African-American students from area universities, colleges and seminaries, including John Lewis, Diane Nash, Marion Barry, James Bevel and Bernard LaFayette. There were a few European-American students who joined the protests including Candie Anderson who was at Fisk University as an exchange student.

As Diane Nash recalls, the waitresses were very nervous, as were the students doing the sit-in: "They [waitresses] must have dropped two thousand dollars' worth of dishes….We all worked very hard not to laugh, even though I was wall-to-wall terrified." (Diane Nash quoted in Pete Seeger and Bob Reiser, *Everybody Says Freedom: A history of the civil rights movement in songs and pictures* (New York: W.W.Norton, 1989) 30).

John Lewis explains: "You put on your Sunday clothes, and we took books and papers to the lunch counter, and we did our homework, trying to be as dignified as possible. I drew up these rules, like: 'Show yourself friendly at the counter at all times. Sit up and face the counter. Don't strike back or curse back if attacked. Don't laugh out. Don't block entrances.' And it ended with something like 'Remember the teachings of Jesus, Gandhi, Martin Luther King. God bless you all." (John Lewis quoted in *Everybody Says Freedom*, 30)

Candie Carawan [formerly Candie Anderson] recalls:
"About eighty of us went down to the lunch counter that day, fifty girls and about thirty boys. Two girls and three boys were white. I still remember how neatly we all dressed. The idea was to go just as well dressed, as dignified, as you could. The girls in their white blouses and pleated skirts, and the boys with their suits; some of them even had a Bible under their arms. There were fourteen seats at the lunch counter. Fourteen of us sat down. Right away the toughs started throwing things over us and pouring catsup in our hair; putting out cigarette butts on our backs. I've got to say that didn't surprise me. What did surprise me was that when the police came they

just watched. Finally they turned to the students at the lunch counter: 'OK, you-ll nigras, get up from the lunch counter or we're going to arrest you.' When nobody moved, they just peeled those people, with their neat dresses and their Bibles, right off their seats and carried them out to the paddy wagons. Before they were out of the store, another fourteen of us took their places at the counter. They got peeled off, and another fourteen sat down. By the end, eighty of us got arrested. Boy, it was something!" (Candie Carawan, *Everybody Says Freedom*, 30-31)

As momentum grows among students, Highlander Folk School in Tennessee, the school that had played a role in cultivating the convictions and ideas of Martin Luther King Jr., Ralph Abernathy and Rosa Parks just before the Montgomery Bus Boycott began, held its annual meeting of student activists, and focused on this new generation of activists. As they had done during the labor movement and the very early civil rights movement, discussion leaders at Highlander like co-founder Myles Horton, coaxed participants to think through their ideas, goals and tactics carefully and critically. Bernard LaFayette explained:

"Myles Horton loved to play devil's advocate….He was arguing the whole question of why do black and white have to be together. He was saying things like 'Why don't you do something for yourself? What do you have to be with white people?' I had never heard a white man say those things to my face, and he was supposed to be a friend. I got madder and madder. Of course, he was trying to force us to be very clear about what we wanted. I knew what he was doing, but it made me furious. He was always pushing you further; you think you have come to some conclusion about something, and there he is, pushing out the walls, and you have to reach out and grab something. That's what a good teacher does—keeps making you rearrange the blankets to make room for broader ideas." (Bernard LaFayette quoted in *Everybody Says Freedom*, 35)

Carawan also recalls the discussions at Highlander:
"I remember one workshop we had on tactics. The subject worked its way around to going to jail. What good was it, what did it accomplish? Myles [Horton] was playing devil's advocate. That's how he worked—he didn't try to push any idea, he just kept asking questions, making us clarify our thinking. By the end of the discussion we came to the conclusion that if we wanted to make jail part of our tactic, we'd have to be willing to stay in. Otherwise, we'd just be draining our resources in bail money, without tying up the opposition at all. That's the tactic the whole movement used after that." (Candie Caraway quoted in *Everybody Says Freedom*, 34-35)

An example of this tactic came in January 31st, in 1961, when students at Friendship Junior College in Rock Hill, South Carolina, led by CORE field secretary Tom Gaither, conducted a sit-in at a local McCrory's store, attempting to order burgers and coffee or coke. Once arrested, they were sentenced to either thirty days of hard labor on a chain gang, or a 100 dollar each fine. They had decided beforehand to choose "jail, not bail" so that their money would not before added funds supporting the local government's segregationist policies. Instead, their time in jail, while not a walk in the park for them, would tax some of that local government's resources. Gaither and others saw the economic benefit in this, but also saw it as a way of invigorating the movement which had, by that time, lost much of the momentum that had gathered during the previous Spring.

They were sent to a York County Prison Farm for 30 days of hard labor shoveling dirt and snowy gravel for a road drainage ditch project. Soon, however, they were joined by four students from the newly formed Student Nonviolent Coordinating Committee (SNCC). During their jailtime, several of the protesters are put in solitary confinement for refusing to stop singing freedom songs. The Sunday after they arrived at the prison, hundreds of people lined the road near the prison to watch and show support for the Friendship Nine. The local NAACP leader Rev. Cecil Ivory, SNCC-founder Ella Baker, European-American activist Connie Curry of the National Student Association (NSA) and CORE field secretary James T. McCain attended the first gathering of supporters and planned for future meetings. Picketing of the McCrory's store gained people and press coverage. Other jails in the South began to fill as people adopted the new "jail, not bail" tactic. People were drawn to the protesters who were willing to do hard labor for their cause.

Freedom Rides

Fresh from the Rock Hill protest and thirty days hard labor, CORE field secretary Tom Gaither discusses the idea of a new Freedom Ride with fellow CORE field secretary Gordon Carey. They agree to take up the idea with CORE leadership, and plans begin. The 1961 Freedom Ride would be modeled on the 1947 Ride of Reconciliation which had been organized by CORE and the Fellowship of Reconciliation (FOR).

1947 CORE, FOR, and the Journey of Reconciliation

In 1947, CORE and FOR members protested segregation by traveling by bus through the upper South. African-American members sat in the 'white' section and European-American members sat in the 'black' section. All twelve of the riders are eventually jailed, but the ride does not generate much support or media interest.

1961 Freedom Ride

Like the sit-ins, the idea of a freedom ride was partly based on the conviction that a nonviolent protest of unjust policies and laws would not only change laws, but hearts as well. But the 1961 Freedom Ride was also an effort to persuade federal and state governments to enforce the Supreme Court's 1960 decision, *Boynton v. Virginia*, which declared local laws enforcing segregation had no authority on interstate travel, or on places which directly serviced that travel. The ruling looked to the Interstate Commerce Act of 1887 which had interpreted the Constitution to give regulatory power to the federal government regarding commerce, applying it to commerce on railroads, particularly. With all of the contention about railroad travel, some had accused railroads of unfair practices which discriminated against people, especially those who had criticized individual railroad companies themselves.

One of the first people who volunteered was James Peck, a CORE member of the 1947 Journey of Reconciliation. Other freedom riders were mostly CORE members and two SNCC members. All thirteen freedom riders had a week of training in nonviolent ways to react to being attacked. They role-played being riders and attackers, discussed things, then reversed roles and played it out again.

The plan was to begin in Washington, D.C. and travel South through North and South Carolina, then to Georgia and West through Alabama and Mississippi, ending in New Orleans, Louisiana. As in 1947, European-American riders would sit in the 'black' section of the buses (six riders took a Greyhound bus and seven took a Trailways bus) while African-American riders would sit in the 'white' sections. When the buses stopped, African-American riders would sit in areas designated 'white' and use 'white-only' restrooms, while European-American riders would sit in the 'black' area and use restrooms designated for 'blacks' or 'coloreds.'

The ride began May 4th. While there was some discontentment by locals as they drove, initially, there was not a lot of violence until Rock Hill, South Carolina, where Albert Bigelow and SNCC rider, John Lewis were beaten in the station waiting area by local European-Americans.

Nevertheless, the real trouble did not begin until the buses reached Alabama. The local Ku Klux Klan (KKK) was encouraged by Birmingham Commissioner of Public Safety Commissioner Eugene "Bull" Connor and turned out mobs of people wielding pipes, chains, baseball bats and brass knuckles. Conner did not put police officers at the bus station, citing the Mother's Day holiday as a reason. Both buses were prevented from going much further, though their fates were different to some degree.

One of the buses was boarded by local KKK bearing weapons, at the border of Alabama. The thugs begin to drag African-American riders to the back of the bus. When European-American riders, James Peck and sixty-year old Dr. Walter Bergman asked them to stop, both were attacked: Peck was knocked unconscious and Bergman was kicked in the head repeatedly. The kicking caused a cerebral hemorrhage that confined Bergman to a wheelchair for the rest of his life. When the bus arrived at the station in Birmingham, Peck got off and walked toward the 'black' waiting room, but was attacked by a group of local European-Americans, who kicked him in the head, spilling blood and eventually requiring over fifty stitches to sew up his wounds.

The other bus was attacked by the mob in Anniston, on the border, but its tires were slashed by people using ice picks and knives, so that the bus driver had to pull over just outside of town to change tires. The local mob had followed the bus in cars, pelting it with bricks and bottles, and then attacked again when it stopped. The crowd wanted the freedom riders to come out, but they remained on board. Finally, the crowd decided to hold the doors shut, while someone threw a firebomb inside. People screamed as the bus soon caught fire. The riders would have burned to death had not one of the riders, Albert Bigelow (a former navy captain) forced open the emergency door. The bus did not explode until everyone managed to get out (the crowd had backed off, anticipating the explosion). But then the mob attacked the riders again, beating them repeatedly.

Somehow, they make it to the hospital. Word goes out to Rev. Fred Shuttlesworth, in Birmingham, who organizes several cars of church deacons and members of the Alabama Christian Movement for Human Rights (ACMHR) to drive to Anniston. Around 2AM, hospital staff force the riders to leave, ostensibly because they fear reprisals by a growing mob outside the building. The caravan sent by Shuttlesworth arrives. Though he'd told them to be completely nonviolent and carry no weapons, the deacons secretly took guns with them. They bring the riders to safety. The riders want to continue their journey, but they cannot find any bus drivers willing to drive them. With Attorney General Robert Kennedy urging CORE to let the situation cool off, the riders are taken to the airport and flown to New Orleans, the destination they'd planned when the freedom ride began. In the middle of the night, an angry crowd has to be held off at the airport so that their plane can take off.

While CORE has effectively called off the freedom ride, Nashville members of SNCC had heard about the fate of the ride. They want it to continue, if only to show that violence cannot stop a nonviolent protest. SNCC leader Diane Nash organizes a group of students, calls CORE chairman James Farmer, and convinces him, albeit reluctantly, to allow SNCC members to carry on the ride in place of the injured CORE riders. Farmer knew there would be more violence and feared the young people would be killed. But Nash was insistent, arguing that "'if we let them stop us with violence, the movement is dead! Every time we start a drive, they will just roll in the violence. Your troops have been badly battered. Let us pick up the baton and run with it.'" (Diane Nash quoted in *Everybody Says Freedom*, 52)

Bernard LaFayette, who had wanted to go on the Freedom Ride with his roommate at American Baptist Seminary, John Lewis, had not been able to go because he was twenty and couldn't get his parents to sign the permission slip. They wanted him to stay in school and felt that signing the slip would be like signing a death certificate. But after the buses are attacked, he and others cannot hold themselves back anymore. He recalls: "CORE didn't want our blood on their hands. But we were determined. We felt that we had to continue. The movement was at stake. If you allow a show of violence to stop your movement, then you'll only encourage a violent response every time you do something. A principle was at stake here. Also, we were outraged. They had done such dastardly things to the freedom riders, and the whole nation, from the attorney general on down, seemed paralyzed. It was a very serious decision—my parents were furious—this was the first time we really felt like we were facing death. We might have been drafted to die in a war, like many of our fellow students who were killed in Vietnam. We could have died senselessly in a car accident. The whole question of life and its fullness and its limitations and its value came up. Life is so tenuous. We felt an urgency of making a contribution; we felt like we had been very fortunate to be black and to have been in good colleges in the South, and we felt we wanted to give something back; we owed a debt to leave things better than we found them. On the other hand, if we didn't make our contribution then, while we were in college, we'd be in the working world raising families and buying homes. Very soon we'd have too many obligations. This was the time to make a contribution." (Bernard LaFayette quoted in *Everybody Says Freedom*, 68)

On May 17th, ten SNCC members, including two European-American members as well as the two SNCC members who had been on the first Ride (John Lewis and Hank Thomas), took a bus from Nashville to Birmingham. When they got to Birmingham, they were arrested by Commissioner Conner and jailed, until, tired of hearing them sing freedom songs, he orders them taken by car to the Tennessee border and left on the side of the road. Those who were in good enough condition to walk managed to call the Nashville office of SNCC from a nearby house. The office sends Les Lillard who picks the riders up two hours later and takes them straight back to Birmingham; determined to press on. Once there, they are joined by more riders, so that there are now 19, 16 African-American and 3 European-American. Initially, no bus drivers are willing to take them, fearing for their lives. The riders waited all night at the bus station while being continually harassed by the Alabama Ku Klux Klan. Bernard LaFayette recalls waiting for a bus to take to Montgomery: "That's a principle of nonviolence. Wherever you're stopped, that's where you stay—until you get some results. Well, they stopped all buses going to Montgomery. They knew we'd be on the next one. This was my first time coming in contact with the Ku Klux Klan. They spent the night with us in the white waiting room. In fact, Robert Shelton, the Imperial Wizard, was there. He was this small guy. He was a Baptist minister wearing this black robe, this beautiful black satin robe with this huge serpent on the back of it. A gorgeous thing—almost oriental. Then there were the lower ranks—these guys with these bed sheets on, they looked sloppy and had coffee stains on their sheets and their hoods were all falling down. They didn't look impressive at all. So, all night, while we tried to sleep, they didn't have anything to do but walk around and step on our feet. And they were drinking sodas with ice and when they finished their drinks, they'd drop the ice on us. There were Birmingham police there. They had these long night sticks. They were nodding off too. They were probably working overtime. Every once in a while, you'd hear this clank on this ceramic tile floor and it would echo throughout the bus station, off of the high ceiling; it was like an echo chamber. You'd know a policeman had dozed off and dropped his night stick…. Another thing is, if you had to go to the bathroom, the policemen weren't going to follow you to protect you. If you went in by yourself, the Klan would probably follow you in. So we had to go in a group. When one man had to go, every man went. We made such a large group, the Klan couldn't even get in." (Bernard LaFayette quoted in *Everybody Says Freedom*, 53)

The Kennedy administration, preparing for a summit with Soviet leader Khrushchev, did not want the freedom rides distracting and embarrassing them. They put pressure on Alabama officials to deal with the freedom riders. Initially, it seems, the solution is to give the riders protection on a bus that would drive directly to New Orleans. But that solution goes against the principles of the freedom riders, as LaFayette explains: "That was against everything we'd been trying to do. We were trying to go stop by stop, as ordinary passengers, desegregating the local facilities and meeting with the people in each city as we went. Zipping us straight through to New Orleans in a few hours would have accomplished nothing. We tried to explain that, but Kennedy and the reporters didn't quite get it. They didn't understand that the goal was to desegregate as we went along. They thought the goal was to get to New Orleans. They probably started agreeing with the governor saying these kids are just trying to get killed. It is not always easy to communicate. Anyhow, what we did was buy one-way tickets to Montgomery. That way they couldn't whisk us straight to New Orleans without kidnapping us. They would have to take us to Montgomery." (Bernard LaFayette quoted in *Everybody Says Freedom*, 53-54)

Governor Patterson finally arranges for state police protection and forces Greyhound to provide a bus and driver. On May 20th, state police escort the riders to Montgomery at 90 miles an hour, to try to avoid any possible ambush or sniper fire, and for most of the trip to Montgomery, the freedom riders have police escorts, police and troopers along the highway, and a plane flying overhead. But when they enter Montgomery, the streets are virtually empty, and the police presence disappears. LaFayette explains: "We learned later that they had blocked off the streets around the terminal. Meanwhile, hiding inside the terminal were all these white farmers dressed in overalls, and others in khaki and blue jeans and plaid shirts. There were also a few women sprinkled in the group. They held axe handles, lead pipes, pitchforks, and baseball bats. I can still see the mean pinched looks on their faces." (Bernard LaFayette quoted in *Everybody Says Freedom*, 54)

As the riders get ready to leave the bus, the mob bursts through the terminal doors, as Fred Leonard explains: "And then, all of a sudden, just like magic, white people were everywhere, sticks and bricks. 'Nigger,' they were shouting, 'kill the niggers!!!' I was thinking, if we got off the back of the bus, like they wanted, maybe they wouldn't kill us. Then I decided, No! I'll get off the front and take what's coming!" (Fred Leonard quoted in *Everybody Says Freedom*, 54)

The crowd attacks the reporters who were covering the story first, assaulting them and breaking cameras. While trying to stay together, the riders decide to meet at the First Baptist Church that night, where a meeting has been scheduled. LaFayette explains some of the difficulties: "We tried to get the women into the cabs. There were a few black-run cabs at the terminal. But as soon as the white women got in a cab, the black driver would get out. This was the Deep-South; the drivers were brave enough to drive the freedom riders, but there was a taboo—a black man couldn't drive a white woman. So then we tried to put the black women into the cabs, but they wouldn't go. 'How are we going to look—the black men stay and the white men stay and the white women stay, but the black women leave.' I think that's when I really started to respect women's power." (Bernard LaFayette quoted in *Everybody Says Freedom*, 54)

Without a clear way to escape, the riders try to stay together. LaFayette explains: "Our only hope was to stay together. We joined hands in a circle and started singing We Shall Overcome. The song has different meanings at different times. Sometimes you're singing about the problems all over the world—'We shall overcome'; sometimes you're singing about problems in the local community—'We shall overcome.' But in that bus station it was a prayer—a song of hope that we would survive and that even if we in that group did not survive, then we as a people would overcome. Then the mob broke into the circle and grabbed Jim Zwerg, a student from Appleton, Wisconsin. They all stomped on him and made him the victim because he was white. John Lewis was right next to me when they swung a metal bat at him. Then I saw them grab William Barbee, a student at American Baptist Seminary in Nashville, and throw him down onto the pavement. They had a foot on his neck and they tried to force a lead pipe down his ear." (Bernard LaFayette quoted in *Everybody Says Freedom*, 55)

LaFayette and Fred Leonard are attacked and chased, at one time leaping to a parking lot from fifteen feet above, into a post office where the mob follows them sending mail in every direction. Transportation to the hospital is hard to find; a black ambulance takes one of the riders to a hospital, a black minister takes another in his car, and the only hospital in town willing to treat the riders is the Catholic hospital, St. Jude's. But even in the hospital, injured as they were, the riders vow to continue on.

The riders sneak into Rev. Ralph Abernathy's First Baptist Church dressed as part of the choir, singing with them and never being recognized by the undercover policemen in the church. That night they are taken in by Rev. Shuttlesworth and other members of the church.

The next day, Sunday, May 21st, a meeting is held in honor of the riders at First Baptist Church. Over 1200 people are in the church, but the church itself is surrounded by an angry mob of 3000 European-Americans. Rev. Shuttlesworth has to push through the mob to bring in James Farmer. Farmer recalls: "The streets were full of roving bands of short-sleeved white men, shouting obscenities….The crowds grew thicker as we approached the church….As we got close, they clogged every roadway, waving Confederate flags and shouting rebel yells….As we stopped, the crowds grabbed hold of the car and began rocking it back and forth. We shoved the car into reverse, heavy-footed the accelerator and zoomed backwards….The only approach was through a graveyard, but we were too late, the mob was already there, blocking the entrances to the church. Shuttlesworth just plowed in, elbowing the hysterical white men aside….'Out of my way,' he said. 'Let me through.' The mob obeyed….Looking back, I can only guess it was an example of the 'crazy nigger' syndrome—'Man, that nigger is crazy; leave him alone, don't mess with him.'" (James Farmer quoted in *Everybody Says Freedom*, 58)

The crowd begins to chant 'Freedom, Freedom, Freedom!' louder and louder. In the afternoon, Dr. King arrives and shortly after that he gets a call in the church office from Robert Kennedy, the attorney general, who wants the rides to stop so things can cool-down. He asks Farmer about it and he puts the question to Diane Nash and the other riders. They refuse. Farmer tells Dr. King, "'Tell the attorney general that we've been cooling off for 350 years. If we cool off anymore we'll be in deep freeze.' King smiled: 'I understand.'" (*Everybody Says Freedom*, 60)

There are a few, virtually helpless federal agents present, but no local or state law enforcement. The crowd grows angrier, breaks windows and throws in tear gas. The people inside prepare for the worst, sending children to the basement while some of the adults bring out guns they have brought in. Then the crowd at the back of the church starts making a lot of noise as they find a door through which they can force their way into the basement. Church members start to block the door with whatever they can find, and then put the weight of their bodies on it. The crowd outside pushes too, and the wooden door starts to crack.

Dr. King speaks to the people in the church to offer encouragement, but things look grim. Just as the crowd breaks into the basement, however, 200 U.S. marshals show up with members of the Alabama National Guard. The Kennedy administration had persuaded Alabama Governor Patterson to send in the Guard, but once they drive away the mob, the Guard refuses to allow the people inside the church to leave, holding them in the building at bayonet point, in spite of the tear gas or the fact that the crowd is no longer present and that people are suffering from tear gas.

Some of the riders continuing on to Jackson, ask Dr. King to join them. Dr. King is already on probation for a minor traffic violation (forgetting to change his state driver's license when he'd moved from Montgomery to Atlanta) and has already been jailed because of that and a sit-in he'd taken part in, in Atlanta in October of 1960. Nevertheless, some of the riders are critical of his unwillingness to join them.

The Kennedy administration devises a way to reduce the media coverage that is embarrassing them and the country as a whole. By May 24th, they convince the governors of Mississippi and Alabama to keep the mobs from stopping freedom riders from traveling, but they give the governors free reign to arrest freedom riders for breaking local segregation laws, in spite of the *Boynton v. Virginia* decision.

Nevertheless, more and more freedom riders keep showing up, such as the chaplain of Yale University, William Sloane Coffin, SNCC member Charles Sherrod, Rev. Shuttlesworth, Rev. Abernathy and others. In spite of the Kennedy administration call for a break in the freedom rides, CORE, SNCC and SCLC keep the pressure on all summer by forming the Freedom Ride Coordinating Committee to keep riders coming from June until September.

In most cases, the state governments allowed the riders as far as Jackson, Mississippi. From there, they were arrested and sent to local prisons. When those prisons filled, riders were sent to Parchman Penitentiary where they were held in the maximum security section. They were only allowed to wear underwear and were given no mail.

This kind of treatment became more or less standard for freedom riders that summer. When the riders would not stop singing Freedom songs, their mattresses and sheets were often taken away, so that they could lay on the hot rails and springs. The screens were sometimes removed from their windows so that mosquitoes and other bugs could keep the riders company. In some cases, a truck with pesticide was backed up to the windows and pesticide was sprayed into the cells.

It was not high living, but frightening and transformative, as Cordell Reagon recalls: "We were in the Hinds County jail, and we were fasting and singing all the time. We were in separate cells, but we could sing to each other so it wasn't bad. Suddenly one morning, very early, they come for us and they say, 'Get dressed. You're leaving.' This was Jackson, Mississippi, in 1961. Well—I knew I was going to die. All I saw was these people taking us out in a field and shooting us. I prayed and gave up my life in my mind. They threw us into these big old trucks, really high up, the bed of the truck as high as your head. And we were in there, all thrown together, and it was dark, no ventilation, and we all knew that we were going to get killed. They could kill every black man and black woman among us and it wouldn't even make the papers. I felt so helpless, I became furious. Despite all my nonviolent training, that was when my rage became solid inside me." (Cordell Reagon quoted in *Everybody Says Freedom*, 61-63)

When they get to Parchman penitentiary at 6AM, they are not killed, but put into the cells there. Reagon describes the noncooperation of two, European-American pacifists and the effect it had on everyone there: "The guards start yelling at the guys, 'Git up! Goddamned nigger lover!' and kicking them, and we're not doing anything. They tell them, 'Take off your clothes.' These guys don't move. So, the guards bring over some cattle prods—electric cattle prods—and they start sticking them. They take these cow prods and they start up and down these cat's bodies. These guys are just laying on the floor, their bodies twitching and jerking with the electric shocks, but they don't even make a sound. Finally, they just cut the clothes off these guys and took them away. I'd been through a lot—having cigarettes put out on me, and been hit and bashed—but this day, watching these two men, I lost my fear. It happened to all of us in that jail. We realized we could say to them, 'Kill me—I'm going to love you anyhow. But I am not going to cooperate with you.' We all realized that we were much more powerful than them. That's when we all became noncooperative. We took the mattresses off of our beds, and stood them up against the wall, and slept on a half-inch piece of steel. We fasted and everything. The rednecks did everything they could. Every time they tried to bogart us—they would bash our heads against the wall, everything the could—and we would just keep singing and praying. They could not understand the stuff." (Cordell Reagon quoted in *Everybody Says Freedom*, 63-64)

During those months in 1961, pressure mounted on the Kennedy administration as roughly 450 freedom riders from places like New York, Nashville, Detroit and Knoxville took part in 60 freedom rides in various parts of the South. Finally, the administration conceded and put pressure on the Interstate Commerce Commission (ICC) to enforce the *Boynton v. Virginia* decision, which it did on November 1st, 1961. The new policies effectively desegregated interstate bus travel throughout the country, as well as the eating and restroom facilities which serviced bus travel. The Freedom Rides not only succeeded in getting 'teeth' for the *Boynton v. Virginia* decision, but in encouraging skeptical African-Americans in the rural, deep South, that these protests were not fruitless and could bring about change for the better. As Cordell Reagon remembers, the riders: "shouted and sang and prayed and joked from cell to cell. They changed this prison, and most of all they changed one another." (Cordell Reagon quoted in *Everybody Says Freedom*, 65)

Patriotism, Racism and the Red Scare

Cold War Politics and the Labor Movement
Cold War opposition to communism led to the Red Scare, and anyone critical of the policies of the United States could be labeled an anti-American communist, particularly if they brought up hot-button topics related to communism, such as labor unions and differences of economic class.

While the irony of egalitarian rhetoric against the Nazi's during WWII despite anti-egalitarian government during Segregation may have had some influence on *Brown v. Board of Education*, surely the continued irony of internal segregation despite opposition to oppression in the Soviet Union was an ongoing factor in the desire of some of our country's leaders to see segregation addressed in some manner. How could we have the moral standing to call for other countries to become more democratic when we tolerated practices of harassment that discouraged participation in democracy at home.

Various unions and groups working to help the laboring poor, on farms or in cities, were equated with communists during the years of the red scare, though the majority were just fighting for the rights and dignity of hard-working people from a variety of minority groups and/or from the working poor. The Highlander Folk School in Tennessee had begun working with the Labor movement and was opposed by many as communist. Their work was dedicated to helping people help and learn from each other, regardless of which ethnic group they came from, and they regarded such interaction as a higher commitment to democracy than most people exhibit. We can find such a commitment in other groups working for civil rights.

Jewish-American and Latin-American Civil Rights Efforts
People from all ethnic and religious backgrounds participated in the civil rights movement. Jewish-Americans and Latin-Americans were two prominent, minority groups who were involved in the movement.

While Jewish-Americans had experienced discrimination and harassment themselves, they recognized the points of similarity in their struggles and those of African-Americans. We can see Jewish-American involvement in the Civil Right Movement in many ways. A number of Jewish-Americans were active in the NAACP, including one of the co-founders, Dr. Henry Moskowitz. They worked as fundraisers, activists, and lawyers for various civil rights groups. Julius Rosenwald, a Jewish-American philanthropist, provided some or all of the funds for a number of elementary and secondary schools for African-American, as well as for well over a dozen colleges, such as Morehouse, Fisk and Dillard. Stanley Levison, a Jewish-American businessman, worked closely with Dr. Martin Luther King Jr. in SCLC, advising, but also leading fundraising and publicity. Jewish-Americans were also the most prominent minority group members, outside African-Americans, who worked with SNCC .

During the "Freedom Summer" of 1964, a large number of the student activists who came South were Jewish-American. Two, in particular, were members of CORE and worked on Voter Registration in Mississippi. Michael Schwerner (who had worked with CORE in New York, Maryland) with his wife, Rita, had run a CORE field office in Meridian, Mississippi where they set up a community center for African-Americans. Schwerner organized voter registration and also went door to door to try to talk to European-American members of the community. He also organized a boycott of a local store until an African-American was hired. On June 21st, 1964 he, Andrew Goodman, another Jew who worked in the CORE voter registration project in Mississippi, and James Chaney, an African-American activist, drove to Philadelphia, Mississippi to see what was left of the Mt. Zion Methodist Church. That church had been used as a freedom school by CORE, but had been burned down a few days earlier. They never made it back to Meridian, however. Their bodies were found two months later in an earthen dam. After political pressure was applied to the FBI, which had little desire to help, an investigation eventually revealed that local people and local law enforcement had been involved in finding and killing all three after they had been taken into police custody, briefly jailed but refused phone calls, and then released from jail during the night and ordered to drive back to Meridian immediately.

Latin-Americans began to organize for protection soon after the United States annexed lands that had once been part of Mexico. Families suddenly found that they were unwelcome and unwanted on lands that had been theirs for generations. There was discrimination and a form of segregation. Places of business sometimes refused service to Latin-Americans; there were "white-only" water fountains, in some Western states, as well as segregation in education. Latin-American children were deemed inferior to European-American children and were sent to shabby buildings called "Mexican Schools." Voting was also suppressed especially by using the difference in languages (Spanish and English) as a barrier. There were also murders of various kinds and numerous hangings. Prominent among the civil rights groups that formed to address harassment and offer people protection were the Order of the Sons of America, the Knights of America, and the League of Latin American Citizens. Other groups existed, some for longer than others, but in 1927 members of these three larger groups began a two-year effort to merge together. In 1929, despite some differences between strong leaders in each of the groups, the League of United Latin American Citizens (LULAC) formed.

Since then, LULAC worked to help end segregation in restrooms, restaurants, drinking fountains, swimming pools, barber shops and other public places. In 1945, LULAC successfully led a legal effort to compel the Orange County school system to integrate. Then, in 1946, LULAC helped file a court case against segregated schools in California. They were successful initially and also won on appeal to the United States Court of Appeals for the Ninth Circuit, the case of *Mendez v. Westminster School District*, which ruled that the segregation of Mexican and Mexican-American students from other European-American students was unconstitutional. Though LULAC worked this case independently, the NAACP was one of the organizations which filed an *amicus curiae* (friend of the court) brief supporting the argument that segregation in the classroom was unconstitutional. *Mendez v. Westminster School District* became an important precedent for *Brown v. Board of Education*, the ruling that declared the "separate, but equal" doctrine unconstitutional.

Latin-American civil rights groups, did not work closely with civil rights groups outside of the Western United States, though members of both groups saw common cause with one another. There were a few Latin-American activists in SNCC, but most activists focus on geographical areas, and the discrimination and brutality in those areas, closer to home. esp. in California and Texas. They needed to organize farmers and migrant farm workers, who were often discriminated against by employers and also denied the right to vote.

Cesar Chavez, who worked with migrant farm workers and others, was one of the most prominent, Latin-American leaders of the 20th century. After his parents were cheated out of their home in Arizona, the family moved to California to live as migrant workers. They lived in meager conditions and before he could enter high school, Chavez left school to work in the fields to help support his family. He saw the unfair way farm workers were treated and how employers did not seem to care. When he joined the Marines in 1944, he again experienced prejudice and discrimination. Encouraged by a local priest, and inspired by the teachings of St. Francis of Assisi as well as by those of Gandhi, Chavez began working part time for the Community Service Organization branch near home, helping get workers registered to vote. He was quite successful at this, and in time gave up his job picking apricots to concentrate on helping other farm workers. In 1962 he organized what later became the United Farm Workers. Over the years he organized and led nonviolent boycotts, strikes, marches and fasts, aiming to improve the treatment of farm workers, address injustices and unsafe practices, and secure the right of workers to unionize as well as to participate in boycotts.

Realistic Patriotism vs. Complacent Patriotism
Whether their people were living in this land before it became the United States or became annexed to the United States, or whether they were brought here by force, many minority groups in the United States have expressed a patriotism that is distinct from that of other Americans. While there had been efforts to remove African-Americans from the United States and send many back to parts of Africa, such as those of the American Colonization Society, many did not want to leave the country of their families and birth. The nation as a whole had done a cruel injustice to people of African descent, generally, but the hard work and service that they had provided the country, as well as the victories they won (however large or small) in spite of that hardship, connected them with this land. Patriotism was not complacent or naïve from the standpoint of African-American history. You could not deny the injustices, the enslavement, the lynchings, the prejudice, and the social structures that kept you and people of your ethnic group in poverty, and that aimed to demean you and make you think less of yourself. Those injustices were an indisputable part of the experience of African-Americans in America.

At the same time, you could find reason for, and the will to express, a realistic patriotism. Dr. King expressed this realistic patriotism in some of his writings and sermons. In a sermon entitled "The Drum Major Instinct," which he gave in 1968 several months before his assassination, he expressed both the frustration with injustice and the hope and promise of a better America.

First, he explained the propensity of people generally to want to be seen as better than others; to be on top, to have attention because we are regarded as better than others. He saw it as an outgrowth of our human nature to need help and attention, whether for our sustenance or for companionship. Babies cry for food; students in college yearn for new friends.

Dr. King described this instinct as natural enough, but as potentially dangerous, especially in the context of a society in which this instinct for attention and desire to be first and best could be used to fuel consumer buying. Capitalism was built on competition, and where that competition was rampant, it sought to convince people both that the drum major instinct was important, and that it could be solved by simply buying the newest model of car a dealer was selling, or owning the biggest and most lavish home around.

Such competition may seem somewhat innocuous, the inconvenience of trying to "keep up with the Joneses" as we say, but Dr. King pointed out that it led people to feel better about themselves only when they could find an outward way to appear better than other people. This was a double-edged sword, since self-worth is often felt in relative terms: the effort to make yourself appear better was, at the same time, the effort to make others seem worse. In other words, self-worth became a matter of separating and elevating your own perceived importance at the expense of others.

The hope to elevate one's own importance and the fear that one would appear less important in relation to others, both led to tension and contention between various ethnic groups. It did damage to everyone in the process. As Dr. King stated:
> And then the final great tragedy of the distorted personality is the fact that when one fails to harness this instinct, he ends by trying to push others down in order to push himself up. And whenever you do that you engage in some of the most vicious activities. You will spread evil, vicious, lying gossip on people, because you are trying to pull them down in order to push yourself up. ("The Drum Major Instinct" in *A Testament of Hope*, 262)

In a country of diverse ethnic groups, groups already distinguished by a history of unfair hiring practices, unfair housing practices, prejudicial treatment based on religion and ethnicity, and the artificial status distinctions encouraged by slavery, and later by Jim Crow, the drum major Instinct could lead to violence and hatred:
> Do you know that a lot of the race problem grows out of the drum major instinct?
> A need that some people have to feel superior. A need that some people have to

> feel that they are first, and to feel that their white skin ordained them to be first. And they have said it over and over again in ways that we see with our own eyes….And think of what has happened in history as a result of this perverted use of the drum major instinct. It has led to the most tragic prejudice, the most tragic expressions of man's inhumanity to man." ("Drum Major," 263)

When this drum major instinct is misused in such ways, ethnic groups who are 'pushed down' emotionally and financially, will not tend to espouse a complacent and naïve patriotism for the country as a whole. A naïve patriotism would overlook such systemic injustice in favor of putting the larger group first at all costs. That may work for people who have, as a whole, benefitted from the country's unfair treatment of other groups, and the prejudices that have continually disadvantaged those other groups. But if you are a member of one of those groups, your patriotism is not likely to complacently accept such an unfair condition.

Dr. King saw the injustice of our country and would not overlook it. He also saw the injustice in some of our country's foreign policies and refused to overlook it as well. Both stemmed from the drum major instinct, according to Dr. King, and despite the good things about the country, he would not overlook the bad. In the competition of nations, the United States was, as much as Russia and China, risking nuclear war and the widespread destruction of life because of a misuse of the drum major instinct:

> But this is where we are drifting, and we are drifting there, because nations are caught up with the drum major instinct. I must be first. I must be supreme. Our nation must rule the world. And I am sad to say that the nation in which we live is the supreme culprit. And I'm going to continue to say it to America, because I love this country too much to see the drift that it has taken. God didn't call America to do what she's doing in the world now. God didn't call America to engage in a senseless, unjust war, [such] as the war in Vietnam. And we are criminals in that war. We have committed more war crimes almost than any nation in the world, and I'm going to continue to say it. ("Drum Major," 265)

To many in a nation fighting a 'Cold War' with communist countries such as China and the Soviet Union, the equation of the United States with them must have sounded unpatriotic, if not traitorous. To say that a country which had fought fascist nations, losing many lives in the process, which had freed victims of the holocaust, and which provided humanitarian and other aid to war-devastated Europe after the second world war, was committing war crimes may have sounded short-sighted and disrespectful. No doubt Dr. King's further warnings that God would punish America for its injustices would also sound unpatriotic to many. Dr. King explained:

> But God has a way of even putting nations in their place. The God that I worship has a way of saying, "Don't play with me….Don't play with me, Babylon. Be still and know that I'm God. And if you don't stop your reckless course, I'll rise

up and break the backbone of your power." And that can happen to America. ("Drum Major," 265)

European-Americans who had been schooled on the hard-won and justified dominance of America in the world, and who had enjoyed the benefits of that dominance more than African-Americans (or Native Americans for that matter) would find it hard to see past the suggestion that America should not be first among nations. They would likely see it as an attack on the well being, greatness and, what seemed to them like, the legitimate and honorable status of America as leader of the free world. But Dr. King expressed a patriotism and love of country that saw greatness in other terms.

Material greatness was a small kind of greatness from his perspective. It led other nations to envy and try to bring you down. It twisted up the natural strength and determination of the nation's people in self-destructive efforts to push one another down in order to enjoy a false sense of worth and importance. This is a misuse of the drum major instinct, according to Dr. King, and a misunderstanding of patriotism. Realistic patriotism is not complacent, but looks at America honestly, sees the problems and injustices, and then acts in the most generous way to solve and heal them. Healing can be hard and inconvenient, but as Dr. King said, "I love this country too much to see the drift that it has taken." ("Drum Major," 264) and that meant taking action to help. It is a tough love. It is a love that seeks what is best for all, not just some, and Dr. King linked it to the proper use of the drum major instinct, and to the advice Jesus gave James and John, in Mark 10:35-45, when they wanted to have a higher status than the other disciples, and Jesus disagreed:

> He [Jesus] said in substance, "Oh, I see, you want to be first. You want to be great. You want to be important. You want to be significant. Well you ought to be. If you're going to be my disciple, you must be." But he reordered priorities. And he said, "Yes, don't give up this instinct. It's a good instinct if you use it right. It's a good instinct if you don't distort it and pervert it. Don't give it up. Keep feeling the need for being important. Keep feeling the need for being first. But I want you to be first in love. I want you to be first in moral excellence. I want you to be first in generosity. ("Drum Major," 265)

In saying this, Dr. King was responding to critics who had associated him with Communism and other anti-American ideologies. Drawing from American's Christian heritage, Dr. King asserted that America needs to grow to fulfill, as he says, the new definition of greatness that he believed Jesus had set forth:

> And he [Jesus] transformed the situation by giving a new definition of greatness. And you know how he said it? He said now, "Brethren, I can't give you greatness. And really, I can't make you first." This is what Jesus said to James and John. You must earn it. True greatness comes not by favoritism, but by fitness. And the right hand and the left are not mine to give, they belong to those who are prepared. And so Jesus gave us a new norm of greatness. If you want to

> be important—wonderful. If you want to be recognized—wonderful. If you want to be great—wonderful. But recognize that he who is greatest among you shall be your servant. That's your new definition of greatness. ("Drum Major," 265)

Dr. King was saying that America and Americans will become great in the higher sense that Jesus articulated once we face our problems realistically and work together to fix them. As such, it is a realistic patriotism.

Dr. King believed that everyone was being hurt by the present system. He described one of the conversations he had with European-American guards during one of his many stays in jail. They wanted to debate Dr. King's position on segregation. They believed segregation was good. Over several days, he calmly discussed matters with them. After this, Dr. King began to realize just how these guards lived. They did not have more money or material wealth than many African-Americans; many of the guards lived in similar material circumstances. As he said:

> And when those brothers told me what they were earning, I said, now "You know what? You ought to be marching with us. You're just as poor as Negroes." And I said, "You are put in the position of supporting your oppressor. Because through prejudice and blindness, you fail to see that the same forces that oppress Negroes in American society oppress poor white people. And all you are living on is the satisfaction of your skin being white, and the drum major instinct of thinking that you are somebody big because you are white. And you're so poor you can't send your children to school. You ought to be out here marching with every one of us every time we have a march."…Now that's a fact. That the poor white has been put into this position…he is forced to support his oppressors, and the only thing he has going for him is the false feeling that he is superior because his skin is white. And can't hardly eat and make his ends meet week in and week out. ("Drum Major," 264)

In this, he suggested that a complacent patriotism is so focused on keeping one's status higher than that of another, that it fails to make an evenhanded judgment of one's own status. Dr. King and others believed that America could be so much better than it was if people only began to see the interrelated problems of race, economic status and a distorted desire to be regarded as great. In this sermon, Dr. King expressed the patriotism of many minority groups; a passionate but realistic patriotism.

The Black Church

Historical Roles of Religion in Black America

When Christians were being persecuted by order of the Roman Empire, they were sometimes asked to make an offering to a Roman god, or call the emperor "Lord" and thereby endorse the view that a man, the emperor, was a god. Their Christian beliefs in only one God, and the great conviction many had in that belief, tied to their faith the saving power of Jesus, led many of them to refuse to outwardly support religious views and/or practices that were not their own. Often, Christians were also used as scapegoats for disasters and other bad times for the Empire. Even when Christianity had become more accepted, and even endorsed, by the Empire, theologians such as St. Augustine had to defend the view that bad times were a result of turning to Christianity and away from the Pagan gods of Roman heritage. Christians defended their obedience to God above their obedience to any human ruler.

It is then ironic that while white churches in America sought to bring Christianity to people of African descent, the message they taught was one of obedience to the ruling white society, and to one's slave master in particular. Somehow, they tried to make it sound like this was what God wanted; they found statements in the Bible about people keeping slaves, which they used to justify the practice of slavery in America. While some white American may have been well meaning in their intentions to help save the souls of black Americans, surely others saw aspects of their religion as a useful tool for controlling black Americans, whether slave or freed person. Those with such an irreligious purpose for their preaching would point to Noah and the curse he put to the people of Ham, and used that as evidence for the inferiority (intellectual and moral) of black Americans. Because of this, they argued, white Americans had a religiously sanctioned duty to rule over black Americans, and a religiously sanctioned superiority as well. For people who were determined to use whatever means were necessary to keep black Americans either in slavery, or (after slavery ended) in a condition of virtual servitude, Christian teachings, if used selectively, were a powerful means to that end.

One of the main problems with this endeavor was the violence and cruelty of slavery itself, which was difficult to justify to the person to whom such violence and cruelty was being done, regardless of how many places you can find a reference to slavery in the Bible. Slaves could be forced to go to the white churches and listen in a respectful way to the sermon; but the mind of a man or woman cannot so easily forget hardship and anguish, and the heart of a man or a woman is not so easy to force. It has its own beat; its own rhythm.

Another problem was cultural and religious in nature. While black Africans had been forcefully abducted from their homelands with little more than their own clothing, they could not be easily stripped of the cultural and religious practices in their hearts and minds. Songs, rhythms, and religious practices were important aspects of culture that people cherished and valued, not just as cultural identifiers of the past, but as healing practices of the present. And black Americans, before and after slavery was abolished, needed healing because of the horrible conditions in which they were forced to live.

When the slave trade was ended in the early 19th century, slaves who were born in America were cut off from new slaves from Africa many of whom would be closer to their African heritage. But they did not forget about their religious background. The practices and songs began to change and respond to the conditions of life that people were facing. Even if they began to use English words and references to elements of Christianity, the songs, rhythms and practices associated with traditional, African religious life continued to live. Songs with shouting and clapping were sung, despite attempts by white society to ban them, as were songs sung with moaning. These ways of singing and worshipping often led to intense and ecstatic religious experiences.

In secret meetings called "hush harbors" people of African heritage shared their religious practices and developed ways to blend those practices with Christian teachings. While Christian ideas of heaven were certainly part of their beliefs, the idea of a spiritual home was mirrored by the idea of an earthly home away from the life of slavery and racism. Religious songs, spirituals such as "Wade Into The Water" and "Swing Low Sweet Chariot," were often coded with words about places to run to and ways to escape from slave-catchers. The attempt of the community to cope with and/or escape from the life of servitude and violence became part of the black community's religious life, and this was reflected in the early black churches.

Black churches in the North and South had some differences in the years after slavery was ended. The Northern churches generally put more emphasis on a religious practice with calm, reasoned religious study of church teachings. The Southern black churches had infused Christianity with elements of African religious practice, including energetic singing, dancing and drumming. Black churches in the North and South, however, differed from the white churches, in that the church was a refuge from the persecution black Americans continued to experience, as well as a place to voice calls for justice and make plans to try to bring about some level of social justice.

During the Civil Rights Movement, it was natural that black churches and church leaders would play a huge role in leading various activities. Black ministers were already expected to give voice to the suffering of members of the community, as well as to call for actions to alleviate that suffering. Comparing Southern governments to Egypt, it was natural for preachers to call for them to "Let my people go!" In the context of expressing the pain of those listening to their sermons, they would express frustration and anger at white America. To white Americans, however, rhetoric of this kind would be interpreted as unpatriotic, at the very least. In the 1950s, as the Red Scare became more and more prominent in American life, the expression of frustration and anger in black churches would only fuel suspicions that preachers and members of their congregations were communists trying to overthrow democracy and the American way of life. Sermons declaring the unfairness of life after Emancipation and the need for economic help, when former slaves were free and yet given nothing with which to start a life, also sounded like a condemnation of free-market capitalism and a call for communism, from the perspective of some white Americans, especially in the South. Yet, for a community that sent its sons to wars to fight for America, only to see them return to persecution, prejudice and violence, such frustration was natural and needed to be spoken by community leaders.

Social Gospel Movement
The Social Gospel Movement was a religious movement in Protestant Christianity, which influenced actions and policies in the 19th century, early 20th century and again in the 1950s and 60s in the civil rights movement. Theologically, the movement is based on post-millennialist views which believed that the second coming of Jesus Christ would only come after a period of time during which Christian ethical convictions are applied to society generally to combat social evils such as poverty, crime, discrimination, disease, addictions to destructive substances, ignorance and injustice. Combatting such evils meant that people would have to work for the benefit of others in society, usually those most needy at the bottom of the socio-economic order.

Such altruistic conduct is also, secondarily, connected with bringing about, by human means, a religious event of the greatest importance for believers. Such believers, however, do not need to force people to believe their views on religion, but only to try to help others by combating the social evils mentioned. These post-millennialist views differ in a practical sense from pre-millennialist views. Pre-millennialist views, which were found more in the Southern United States than in the North, argue that Christ's second coming is going to happen soon, and so our energies should be focused on our own personal conduct. Fighting social evils is fine, but because the second coming is so close, they argue, we are better served by working on our own problems, instead of those of others. Social problems take a lot of time to solve.

Post-millennialist views, generally, argue for Christians to take a more active role in public life, but there are important differences even here. Revivalist post-millennialist views aim to help people directly, working with the problems they currently have and trying to help them overcome whatever they are suffering. By working at the grassroots level, revivalist post-millennialists believe that they can transform people's habits and states of character, and thereby also transform society's customs and practices from the bottom-up. Reconstructionist post-millennialists, on the other hand, believe that while grassroots change is fine, there needs to be fundamental change at the larger, political level. The Reconstructionist post-millennialists take a more top-down approach to helping others in society. By taking political control of society, they believe they can more effectively help others. Their way of understanding help, however, asserts that holding all people to the religious laws about conduct in Christianity is a valid way to help them.

In the US, social gospel views were prominent in the Progressive movement and New Deal administration of President Roosevelt. The views and practices of Walter Rauschenbusch typify the social gospel movement in America. These views imply that getting yourself to heaven is not as important, or as pious, as acting ethically to help others, and that Christ's remission of Original Sin is more about loosening the hold of socially harmful habits on us, rather than just absolving our personal sins.

Black Preachers
The concerns and commitments of those advancing the Social Gospel Movement paralleled those of the African-American clergy, though it may not be immediately clear. Further tension between white and black Americans can be linked to the unique character of the preaching style in black churches, and the effect on the congregations. A preacher might begin with a verse or teaching, explaining it and then relating it to contemporary life. But then the preacher would begin to speak in a chanting style of delivery. As he did so, the members of the congregation would respond to his statements and questions, shouting out simple but heartfelt responses, e.g. "yes," "no," "say it," and "Amen!" As this continued, emotions began to run high for the congregation, and often for the preacher. Then, the preacher would often begin to sing and the singing would further stir the feelings of the audience to great intensity. For white Americans not familiar with the roots of black American religious experience in the "hush harbors" and elements of African spirituality, this display of emotion was not only different from the more quiet and reserved character of church services for many white Americans, it was disturbing. To those who also bought into the idea that black Americans were naturally inferior and had to be controlled, these sermons could look like the fires of black insurrections.

During the civil rights movement, the fears of European-Americans that African-American institutions were unpatriotic and possibly communist, were given further strength as churches became the focal point for Movement activities. The church buildings themselves were, often, the only places in the black community where large groups of people could meet to discuss civil rights issues and plan protests. During evening meetings, which were often more singing than planning or speaking, police were sometimes present, keeping track of who was there. Church leaders, such as Martin Luther King Jr., were labeled as communists when they attended workshops, such as those at the Highlander Folk School, a school which was associated with the labor movement. But in the end, these people and groups, from many ethnic and religious backgrounds, were putting their lives on the line to act patriotically for a better America, a more perfect America, and an America become a beloved community.

Appendix III:
Introduction to Highlander Folk School:
The Struggle for Real Democracy in Appalachia

Opening Narrative

"It was in that same strike that they tried to run me out of town. One Sunday at about four o'clock in the morning there was a knock at my hotel door, and a young fellow who was a theological student at the University of the South in Sewanee—he had been to Highlander, but I hadn't known he was in Lumberton—came in and said, 'Myles, I have to see you.' When I asked him what he was doing in Lumberton, he said, 'Well, I'm a summer pastor at the Episcopal church here and I just have to talk to you. Tomorrow at eleven-thirty all the ministers in the mainline churches are going to pray that you're removed from this town. I just couldn't sleep, I had to tell you. They're determined to get rid of you.' To make a long story short, the communication lines to God broke down somehow, and I was still there the next day, so the mill owners decided they'd better try something a little more immediate and they hired some people to kill me. It sounds dramatic, but if you know the labor movement at that time, you know people were killed. The killers came in the middle of the week to the busiest part of town during the busiest time of day, right across from the courthouse. One of the windows in my hotel room on the second floor looked out on the main street. All at once it was very quiet. I looked out the window and I couldn't see anything, couldn't see anybody. When I had gone out at noon to eat lunch, everything was just as busy as it always was. 'Is this Sunday?' I asked myself. 'This is the middle of the week, what's happening?' I went from window to window to see if I could figure out what was going on. Then a car drove up under my window. I couldn't miss that car, because it was the only thing out there moving. There were four people inside, two in the front seat and two in the back. I just stood there and looked at them, and they looked up at me. Finally, one of them said, 'We're coming to get you.' 'Fine,' I said. They nudged each other, took a swig of beer—there were taunting me, so I knew they were the killers. This was it. The week before, a Holiness minister who was one of the union leaders came to my room and asked me if I had a pistol. I told him I didn't, and he said, 'Well, you know there are all these threats about. You'd better keep this pistol.' It was a great big one, and I just put it in the drawer. 'It's loaded, six shots,' he told me, and he left some more shells. I hadn't fired a pistol in years....I could use a rifle, but I had never learned to shoot a pistol. I walked over and got that pistol and walked to the window with it in my hand, and those four men looked at me and looked at each other. One of them said, 'What good is that going to do?' 'Well, I'd like to talk to you a minute, ' I said. 'You know I like to organize.' 'Yeah, but your organizing days are over.' 'Well, the last thing I'd like to do is to try to help somebody get organized.' They laughed, and I said, 'You know you guys need to get organized.' 'Why do we need to get organized?' one of them asked. 'Well, somebody's going to come in this door,' I said. 'You're going to get the key down at the desk.' The hotel was owned by the company. 'You're going to come up here and one guy's going to open that door and come in. And,' I said, 'I'm going to kill the first person that comes in. Next, another person is going to come in and I'll probably kill that person. When the third person comes in, it'll be a toss-up whether I kill him or he kills me. And the last person, he'll be able to kill me. There's no question about that. You've got to decide which ones of you I'll kill. I don't have a problem—I'm going to be killed—but you've got to decide which ones of you are going to be killed.' Of course you always know that such people think like a mob. They don't think individually. That's why the Klan is brave, that's why all mobs are brave. You've got to personalize it so they understand it's them. I asked one of the men in the front seat, 'You have kids?' 'What's that to you?' he asked. 'Well, if you have,' I said, 'you don't want to die.' I asked everyone if they had kids, and I held the pistol in my hand to emphasize the message, playing one against the other. I said, 'Hey, you in the back seat. Are you going to be dead in a few minutes? Or are you the one who's going to have to haul this guy in the front eat home? What are you going to tell his wife when you get there?' I just kept personalizing it, going round and round individualizing so that they'd think of themselves. Then I told them, 'That's why you need to get organized. You've got to vote on who's going to die. Are you people in the front seat going to die, or are you two in the back seat going to be the ones? Or one in the front, one in the back? Who's going to die?' I never asked, 'Who's going to kill me?' I asked, 'Who's going to die?' They were sure they were going to kill me—that's why they were so brave—but they hadn't thought about themselves. In the meantime, I was standing there with this big old sheepleg (that's what we called pistols), and I had the temptation to twirl it around as they do in the movies, but I was afraid I'd drop it. Finally they muttered to each other and just drove away."[13]

  While the civil rights movement had strong roots in the struggle against slavery and lynching, some of the character and impetus for the movement after 1954 came from a small folk school in the heart of Appalachia. The *Highlander Folk School*, founded by Myles Horton and Don West in 1932, with the encouragement of many and the financial help of Tennessee educator and suffragist Lillian Johnson, began as an attempt to put into practice the faith that people who are struggling in their lives can find the answers to their troubles by talking and working with other people. In rural Tennessee, that meant helping mountain folk, known at the time as Highlanders, connect with and learn from one another, as they struggled to survive as farmers and miners. It meant working with unions and organizing people, and it also meant being labeled "communist" and "atheist" and putting your life on the line. But Myles Horton, the principle mover behind Highlander, was tough, disciplined and deeply in love with the mountain folks he came from in Tennessee. He had a quiet confidence, a determination to act with dignity and treat others respectfully, and he was genuinely curious about people and their potential to help each other and learn from each other. In this introduction to the *Highlander Folk School* module, we will let Myles Horton speak for himself, in most cases, since it emphasizes the importance of life-experience over academic commentary, in a way that parallels the playing of an academic game itself.

---

[13]   Myles Horton, *The Long Haul: an autobiography*, with Judith Kohl and Herbert Kohl (New York: Doubleday, 1990) 123-125

Highlander Folk School: The Struggle for Real Democracy in Appalachia

Subchapters

1) History of Highlander Folk School
2) Religious Influences on Horton and Highlander
3) The Struggle that is True Education
4) True Education is not Training for the Status Quo
5) How True Education is cultivated at Highlander
6) Highlander's Goal: Real Democracy

Detailed Breakdown of Sections:
1) History of Highlander Folk School
    A. Ozone, Tennessee and Vacation Bible Schools
    B. New York and Reinhold Niebuhr
    C. Chicago and Hull House
    D. Denmark and the Folk School Movement
2) Religious Influences on Horton and Highlander
3) The Struggle that is True Education
    A. Faith in People Where They Are
    B. The Role of Conflict in Education
    C. Struggle and Growth for People Already Struggling
    D. Struggle and Nonviolence
    E. Nonviolence in True Education
4) True Education is not Training for the Status Quo
5) How True Education is cultivated at Highlander
    A. A Fluid Method or No Method at All
    B. "First Enliven, then Enlighten": The Importance of Music at Highlander
    C. Holistic and Service-oriented Approach of Highlander
    D. Trust, Compassion, Respect, and Awareness
    E. Learning Circles: the Lack of Hierarchy
    F. Grassroots Leadership: the Lack of Charismatic Leaders

6) Highlander's Goal: Real Democracy and Social Change

1) History of Highlander

A. Ozone, Tennessee and Vacation Bible Schools

During the summer before his senior year at Cumberland University in 1927, Myles Horton worked organizing vacation Bible schools as part of a Student YMCA Summer Program.

He had been frustrated by the Jim Crow traditions of segregation, sometimes violating them by organizing integrated events, and was determined to fight segregation. Most importantly, however, he had become even more aware than previously of the poverty and hardship that people were experiencing in the parts of Tennessee that he worked. He couldn't see how the work he'd been sent to do, encourage people to memorize parts of the Bible and sing hymns, would help people in any meaningful manner. People did not have good jobs or good schools; it was harder and harder to put food on the table.

Horton had no idea how to help these people, but finally, near the town of Ozone, Tennessee, he decided to try. He asked parents of the children going to the Bible schools to come to the church that night to talk about the problems they were trying to deal with. As one commentator explains:

"To his amazement, they came. Some walked through the dusk for several miles down the hollows, knowing they would have to go home in the dark. The things they talked about were basic. How could jobs be found? How does a person test a well for typhoid? Could the once-beautiful hillsides ever grow trees again? At first, they shared what they knew with each other. Horton's inability to answer most of their questions didn't bother them. Soon, however, they started asking him to find someone who did have the answers. The county agent was helpful. So was a man who knew how to test wells."[14]

His work raised some eyebrows as it drew more and more people. His church supervisors said that no one had reported numbers of people that high in that area. When meetings began, people were a bit reluctant to talk, so Horton found someone to sing local songs or tell local mountain stories. These songs and stories from their own culture soon made them more at ease talking. The only experts there were people with expertise in their own problems; but when they shared those problems, they often found answers right in their own area.

People knew that Horton cared about them, and even though he didn't have all of the answers himself, he could help them find the answers they needed, and that was special. By the end of the summer; the didn't want him to leave. One even suggested that if he stayed, he could use her home for all future meetings. Horton wanted to continue helping, but this new way of teaching, getting people to talk to each other and solve their own problems, needed more head-scratching on his part. He left for Cumberland University, but promised to come back.

Horton became the secretary of the student YMCA after he graduated from Cumberland University in 1928. As he traveled around, he continued to read and observe how various schools taught, but found nothing that he felt would help mountain people like those he'd meet in Ozone. He was impressed by the thought of American philosophers William James and John Dewey, which suggested that emotions and reason could work together to change society for the better. Nevertheless, he was finding that some traditions and prejudices in society were preventing that change from happening or even being discussed:

---

[14] Frank Adams, *Unearthing Seeds of Fire: The Idea of Highlander*, with Myles Horton (Winston-Salem, NC: John F. Blair, publisher, 1975) 3

"Horton may have been growing in his personal understanding of the underpinnings of liberal educational philosophy, but his work for the YMCA was out of kilter with time, place, and custom. Everywhere he went as secretary, the meetings he organized were interracial. This caused ripples in colleges, arched some eyebrows in high schools, and raised angry hackles in public places. Horton had an innocent's faith that the YMCA's statement of purpose obligated him to undertake such work: 'The Young Men's Christian Association is a worldwide fellowship of men and boys united by common loyalty to Jesus Christ for the purpose of developing Christian personality and building a Christian society.' Complaints about Horton's activity reached his employers with increasing volume and velocity. They were as pleased to have him resign as he was to leave."[15]

B. New York and Reinhold Niebuhr

Horton realized that he needed help to create something helpful for the mountain people he had lived with and felt so attached to. The colleges and schools around him were not giving him that help; nor were the people of the YMCA, despite a statement of purpose that suggested they should. He got some good advice, however, from a Congregationalist minister, the Reverend Abram Nightingale, who told Horton that he needed to study at Union Theological Seminary in New York. Nightingale had to push Horton, even get him an application, but in the end Horton found his way to the seminary, not with the intention of entering the clergy, but to clarify his own ideas and hear others. One person he studied with, who eventually helped him generate support for the school that would eventually be called Highlander Folk School, was the theologian Reinhold Niebuhr, who was teaching at Union when Horton arrived.

Horton seemed to get along well with Reinie (as he and others called him) and there was a sense that each valued the other highly. Niebuhr once insisted that Horton to take an advanced class with him, though Horton didn't have the prerequisites. He had difficulty understanding Niebuhr at first, and almost dropped the course, explaining that he couldn't understand the lectures and needed more background. When other, well-educated students overheard him telling Niebuhr this, they admitted that they were also having trouble; and this helped convince Horton to stay. As Horton puts it: "Later Reinie would ask me right in the middle of the class, 'Myles, do you understand what I'm talking about?' I was his barometer. The others were ashamed to say they didn't understand. I had no pride. I was there to learn, and I wasn't even worried about grades or credit. All I wanted was to understand, to know."[16]

Horton never forgot why he was in New York; it was because of that experience in Ozone, Tennessee. His desire to learn was always, it seemed, tempered and guided by the need to be able to apply what he learned to the challenges of the mountain people he'd left behind. As he says, "I went to Union because I had problems reconciling my religious background with the economic conditions I saw in society. Reinie later wrote a book called *Moral Man and Immoral Society*, in which he talked about society being immoral, and about people being moral and how

---

[15] Adams, *Seeds*, 9-10
[16] Horton, *Haul*, 35

they can live in an immoral society, exactly my problem. I was moral and society was immoral. I wanted to see if I could get help on my ethical ideas."[17]

The following quotation from *Moral Man and Immoral Society*, speaks to the antagonism of other-worldly moral requirements espoused by religions and this-worldly moral requirements generated in the social environment around us:

"If we contemplate the conflict between religious and political morality it may be well to recall that the religious ideal in its purest form has nothing to do with the problem of social justice. It makes disinterestedness an absolute ideal without reference to social consequences. It justifies the ideal in terms of the integrity and beauty of the human spirit. While religion may involve itself in absurdities in the effort to achieve the ideal by purely internal discipline, and while it may run the peril of deleterious social consequences, it does do justice to inner needs of the human spirit. The veneration in which a Tolstoi, a St. Francis, a crucified Christ, and the saints of all the ages have been held, proves that, in the inner sanctuary of their souls, selfish men know that they ought not be selfish, and venerate what they feel they ought to be and cannot be."[18]

Horton was impressed by the emphasis on reorganizing society to help those most in need. His need for 'background' took him to the library (as it had done at Cumberland) where he read voraciously. He was not out to become an advocate for this or that philosophy or social movement, however. He read works by socialists, communists, advocates and critics of the social gospel movement, pragmatists such as James and Dewey, and educational reformers such as Eduard Lindeman and Joseph Hart, all with an eye toward developing a way to bring about education that could reorganize society in a way helpful to folks such as the mountain people of Ozone. As he tried to find real life examples of these approaches, teaching institutions he found were either too focused on urban and national problems and approaches, or too caught up in internal bickering, to be helpful for mountain people and their real life situations. His readings of black poets and authors helped further his convictions to help all poor, struggling people, regardless of ethnic background.

C. Chicago and Hull House

His commitment kept him from following those who wanted him to join the clergy or become an academic. As he explained, "I didn't go to Union Theological Seminary in New York with the intention of becoming a minister. I went to learn things that would be useful when I returned to the mountains. That was the same reason I went to the University of Chicago the next year."[19] He spent a year at the University of Chicago studying sociology in classes with Dr. Robert Park. He wanted to better understand the positive aspects of conflict:

---

[17] *Ibid.*, 35
[18] Reinhold Niebuhr, *Moral Man and Immoral Society: A Study in Ethics and Politics* (New York: Charles Scribner's Sons, 1932) 263
[19] Horton, *Haul*, 46

"I had been reading about conflict, trying to understand how fundamental change could develop through education in a situation of inequality. I wasn't interested in resolving conflicts that would leave the same people in control and the same people powerless. I discovered almost by accident sociological surveys and papers that hinted at how to deal with these problems, and that there were a number of people in the sociology department at the University of Chicago who were studying social change....I took classes with Robert Park and learned about group problem solving and conflict as a tool for learning. At this time I began to realize that learning which came from a group effort was superior to learning achieved through individual efforts. I also began to understand how to use conflict and contradictions to promote learning."[20]

In addition, he also became familiar with the social conditions and institutions of Chicago. He got to know Jane Addams of Chicago's Hull House. Since the 1880s, Hull House had been a settlement house for immigrants and other working poor people who needed better health, education and culture. His own faith in democratic institutions had been tested by the way competition and prejudice had hampered efforts to reorganize people, but in Addams he found someone who was still optimistic about democracy, or at least democracy in small groups: "Miss Addams' vision of the democratic decision-making process was right out of Horton's rural past. Although she had worked for most of her professional life in the midst of an industrial city and had, in fact, grown up with the rise of industrialization in America, she once told Horton, 'To arrive at democratic decisions, you need to have a bunch of ordinary people sitting around the stove in a country house or store and contributing their own experiences and beliefs to the discussion of the subject at hand. Then you take a poll of the majority opinion of those present, regardless of who they are, and that is a democratic decision.'"[21] Horton explained that Addams said that Democracy was not when a group finds someone else to tell them how to deal with a conflict, but when they debate and decide on a course of action themselves. He was curious where she got the idea for this kind of democracy, and she said it was from her father who'd heard it from Abraham Lincoln himself. Horton was impressed and thought it was good advice. Addams was also a great help with the support network of settlement house directors around the country that Horton developed to get Highlander going.[22]

Horton was equally impressed by the way Addams did not let herself become intimidated by the harassment that was directed at her for her views on war, women's rights and other causes. When he first met her, he bluntly asserted that he wasn't all that interested in what Hull House was doing at present, but in how it got started and in how they handled all of those who harassed her. He had already seen harassment himself and would draw strength from her example.[23]

D. Denmark and the Folk School Movement

---

[20] *Ibid.*, 46-47
[21] Adams, *Seeds*, 18
[22] Horton, *Haul*, 49-50
[23] *Ibid.*, 49

Horton was also inspired by a Danish-born Lutheran minister, the Reverend Aage Møller who had organized folk dances at his Chicago church and opened them to students. He'd heard about Horton's desire to help mountain people through some kind of education, and he suggested that Horton visit Denmark to better see and study the folks schools there. The folk schools of Denmark had begun as an attempt to improve the lives of a people economically and culturally devastated by war:

"Denmark was a ruined nation when the folk schools emerged. Prussia had defeated the Danes for the second time in 1864. The nation was nearly bankrupt. Many Danes were forsaking their native ways, and even their language, to learn German and German customs. For centuries, Danish village life had been rooted in the soil, but by 1964, the church and the schools were calling old traditions pagan. A poet, preacher, and scholar of Scandinavian mythology, Bishop N.S.F. Grundtvig, after nearly a decade of pondering the confusion and misery around him, fashioned a theoretical program for what he called schools of learning. They would be free of traditional forms and methods. They would direct education toward fostering the integrity and natural intelligence of village and farm people."[24]

Grundtvig tried to start such a school in 1844, but could not make it work. Several years later, in 1851, "a shoemaker, Kristen Kold, tried, along with one other teacher and fifteen students, to bring life to Grundtvig's original idea. Kold's school, near the village of Ryslinge on the island of Fyn, was closely connected with the daily lives of the students. No books were used, only the spoken word, and much singing. Kold championed the cause of the peasants in their struggles against landlords, the church, and the nobility. Learning flourished there, and, in the next thirteen years, twenty-six more folk schools opened….The schools were free of government control. There were no grades, ranks, tests, or diplomas. Lectures were limited to Danish history, mythology, religion, and language. Teachers were often young idealists, sensitive to injustices existing in their native land and hopeful for the future. Each folk school had an 'emotionally charged,' clearly-stated purpose."[25] Funding for the schools came in the form of students working at the school, bringing food from local farms and giving what money they could afford. Teachers used music and poetry to motivate. Besides presenting lessons to the students living there, they also gave evening talks for people from the surrounding areas.[26]

Grundtvig's motivations included a recognition that his contemporaries had lost connection with their cultural heritage, and a conviction that while that heritage included historical, mythological and religious stories, beliefs and teachings, it could only be truly 'taught' or passed on to others by direct contact with other people and their way of life, as opposed to book-learning and lecture. Grundtvig called this the 'living word' Grundtvig had come to believe that people could learn from one another, as peers, especially when they shared life

---

[24] Adams, *Seeds*, 20
[25] *Ibid.*, 20-21
[26] *Ibid.*, 21

experiences outside traditional educational settings and the competitive grading methods that were a large part of that experience. As he explained in 1856 at the opening of a folk school: "I saw life, real human life, as it is lived in this world, and saw at once that to be enlightened, to live a useful and enjoyable human life, most people did not need books at all, but only a genuinely kind heart, sound common sense, a kind good ear, a kind good mouth, and then liveliness to talk with really enlightened people, who would be able to arouse their interest and show them how human life appears when the light shines upon it."[27] Some authors have given credit to the folk schools for the determination, grit and solidarity of Danes as they opposed the policies of fascist Germany in the ways they did.

Horton was tempted to go Denmark, for a better assessment of the folk schools, but he had other options. Professor Park had offered him an assistantship in sociology, so he could continue doctoral studies, while the American Missionary Association had offered to put him in charge of a church-sponsored school in Tennessee. The financial considerations were important, but Møller had urged Horton to visit Denmark to find out about the folk schools directly. When Niebuhr supported the idea of visiting Denmark, Horton became committed to going, and after earning enough money, he left in 1931.

Horton traveled around Denmark, sometimes on a bike, visiting various folk schools: "All I lived and learned that year became a part of me. At the time I noted some specifics that might be particularly useful in the future: Students and teachers living together / Peer learning / Group singing / Freedom from state regulation / Nonvocational education / Freedom from examinations / Social interaction in nonformal setting / A highly motivating purpose / Clarity in what for and what against"[28]

Horton's time studying Danish before his trip paid off when he experienced the limitations of translation. "I remember talking to one of the old directors, the son of a founding father of the folk schools, about their early history. He didn't understand that I was more concerned with knowing about the roots of the folk schools and their contribution to greater economic and social democracy in Denmark than with what they later developed into. There's much to learn from how things get started. You can't cut off the top of a tree and stick it in the ground somewhere and make it grow—you have to know about the roots. He kept telling me what I already knew from all the books I'd read. Finally I told him, 'What you're talking about it what Dewey and a lot of other people talked about. That's not what I want to know.' His response was 'Yes, I've been trying to put it in your language.' Immediately I knew why I hadn't been able to get at the roots. I said to him 'Look, my question is limiting you: when you explain this in English, you have to use illustrations you think I'll understand, but I know enough Danish that if you talk slowly, and if you'll be patient with me, I can understand you.' He brightened up instantly, and I plunged right in, just struggling, and he called to his wife, 'Brenda,

---

[27] Steven M Borish, *The Land of the Living: The Danish Folk High Schools and Denmark's Non-Violent Path to Modernization* (Nevada City, California: Blue Dolphin Publishing, Inc., 1991) 18

[28] Horton, *Haul*, 52-53

bring tea, this young man speaks Danish!' As soon as he quit using my language and stopped restricting himself to what he thought I could understand, a whole new world opened up."29

As Horton put it, regarding his talk, in Danish, with a folk school director: "Talking to that old man in his language made Grundtvig's Living Word, which I had only learned about from reading, come alive....[Grundtvig] proposed a School for Life to replace lifeless academic schooling. He believed the experience of the students could be awakened by a search for their roots in Danish history and Norse mythology. The people would find their identity not within themselves but in relationship with others. He also believed that through songs and poetry, students could grasp truths that might otherwise escape them, and that singing in unison was an effective way of inspiring people and bringing them closer together."30

As he traveled, and as his Danish improved, Horton interviewed folk school directors. He found in them a passion to redress injustice and help people see the truth of their own living conditions. They also had a burning desire to turn people's attention to life as it should be, more so than just to life as it is. There were informative elements, but the main focus was on uplifting people's spirits and determination. This is what had impressed him in his studies of Grundtvig himself: "I saw him as a rebel with prophetic insights; a champion and inspirer of the poor and voiceless. I imagined how the terrible economic depression which he experienced at the age of twenty-seven—about my age at the time—must have affected him, just as the depression then paralyzing the United States was affecting me."31

Horton kept notes from each interview and folk school experience as he biked around Denmark. Not every school impressed him; some of the contemporary schools had lost the vitality and clarity of the earlier movement, getting caught up in petty disagreements. But Horton's focus continued to be on his people in the mountains of Tennessee:
"I rode from school to school on my bicycle and later made notes which I labeled 'O' for Ozone, my symbol for reality:...'The job is to organize a school just well enough to get teachers and students together AND SEE THAT IT GETS NO BETTER ORGANIZED. If possible, the school should be on a farm where the scenery is beautiful and there is an opportunity for being alone. Our fellow workers will be selected as students for their ability and direction of their interests. We will consult and share work. Effort will be made to keep them in the ranks of labor, but intelligently so. Go to strike situations and take the students, thus helping labor and education at the same time....The school will be for young men and women of the mountains and workers from the factories. Negroes would be among the students who will live in close personal contact with the teacher. Out of their experiential learning through living, working, and studying together could come an understanding of how to take their place intelligently in the changing world. The school should help people broaden their outlook and acquire definite information by preserving, taking part in and analyzing situations of interest.' I wrote my last

---

29 *Ibid.*, 51
30 *Ibid.*, 51-52
31 *Ibid.*, 52

note in Copenhagen after I had gone to bed Christmas night in 1931: 'I can't sleep, but there are dreams. What you must do is go back, get a simple place, move in and you are there. The situation is there. You start with this and let it grow. You know your goal. It will build its own structure and take its own form. You can go to school all your life, you'll never figure it out because you are trying to get an answer that can only come from the people in the life situation.' I still remember that night. It was the sweetest feeling, a five-year burden had rolled away, and I went back to sleep wondering why it had taken so long. It all seemed so clear and simple—the way to get started was to start. That Christmas night I had rediscovered Ozone."[32]

2) Religious Influences on Horton and Highlander:

While he did not let it get in the way of his conscience or his respect for others, religion was, for Horton, a big part of his life: "Undoubtedly the first book that influenced my life was the Bible, there's no question about that. All my early influences came from the Bible and things like that, you know, not an ultra religious family, but a conventionally religious family, and that was the values in little country towns, you know. You went to church and you went to school. There wasn't anything else to do….There's no question, and I still, the values of the Bible I still hold dear….there's the new Testament and the Old Testament. In the New Testament we learned about love….You can't be a revolutionary, you can't want to change society if you don't love people, there's no point in it. So, you know, love people, that's right out of the Bible. And another thing is, the Old Testament tells primarily about Creation. God was a creator. If you're going to be with people, born in God's image, then you've got to be creators, you can't be followers, you know, or puppets, you've got to be creators. So from the Bible, I guess, people ought to be creative, or live people, people ought to be creative"[33]

Some of his religious conviction came from his family's way of interpreting their Presbyterian background: "Our family was in the Cumberland Presbyterian Church. When the Presbyterians first came into the mountains, they had a very stiff, formal church, but they weren't making much headway because they didn't have enough preachers who knew Latin and Greek. They couldn't compete with the Baptists and Methodists after the great revivals that started in New England came down here, so they started a people's Presbyterian church. Still, they kept all the Calvinist theology, including a belief in predestination: things God preordained to happen would happen. I ran across some of the old theology books in my grandparents' attic and started reading them when I was in grammar school. One day I went to my mother and said, 'I don't know, this predestination doesn't make any sense to me, I don't believe any of this. I guess I shouldn't be in this church.' Mom laughed and said, 'Don't bother about that, that's not important, that's just preachers' talk. The only thing that's important is you've got to love your neighbor.' She didn't say, 'Love God,' she said, 'Love your neighbor, that's all it's all about.' She had a very simple belief: God is love, and therefore you love your neighbors. Love was a

---

[32] *Ibid.*, 53-55
[33] Myles Horton, "The Adventures of a Radical Hillbilly: Part 1" 1981 interview with Bill Moyers, reprinted in the summer 1982 issue of *Appalachian Journal* and subsequently printed in *The Myles Horton Reader: Education for Social Change*, edited by Dale Jacobs (Knoxville, TN: The University of Tennessee Press, 2003) 122

religion to her, that's what she practiced. It was a good nondoctrinaire background, and it gave me a sense of what was right and what was wrong."[34]

It did not bother Horton if some people had the wrong idea about the place of religion in his life: "Well, we were not considered religious by most people because we decided early on that we were going to stay away from all kinds of sectarianism—religious, political, or otherwise. So we didn't have any church or religious affiliation of any kind....But we tried to work with the local community church and did, up until the time that we started getting a number of black students. The church people refused to let them come to the church, and we couldn't very well go without them....We said we wouldn't go without them, so we dropped out of that. We still said that we'd be delighted to take part in any church service or religious service that would allow us to bring out students, but we got no offers....We never said we weren't religious. We just said we weren't church-related."[35]

3) The Struggle that is Education

The story has been told many times in many ways about a youngster watching a butterfly emerge from its chrysalis. There is astonishment at the movement inside the gold-like shelter; there is wonder in the knowledge that a fat, slow caterpillar had spun this structure itself, and transformed, inside, into a beautiful and colorful flyer. But the youngster begins to worry because the butterfly is struggling to escape its chrysalis; the opening seems too small. Filled with reverence for this amazing transformation and feeling connected to it in some way, the youngster resolves to help by taking a knife and carefully cutting a slit so that the chrysalis opening is wide enough for the butterfly to emerge much more easily. The butterfly is not damaged; the youngster has been very careful. The butterfly then emerges, but its head looks awkwardly big and its wings are shriveled. It tries to flutter the wings, but to no avail, and soon, it dies. The youngster is dismayed and feels guilty, but does not understand why. An elder notices, recalls seeing something similar many years ago, and explains to the youngster that the hole in the chrysalis was not too small, it was just right. The head and body of the butterfly were swollen with liquid as it hung in the chrysalis, and the wings needed that liquid if they were to form properly. As it struggled through the small opening, the liquid was forced back and into the compacted wings. This allowed the wings to expand properly and have the strength to carry the butterfly through the air for the rest of its life. Giving the butterfly help, in this instance, was taking away from it the means to grow properly. It's hard to say that all struggle is necessary for growth, but this struggle was necessary for growth. However well-intended, the effort to alleviate the pain of struggle ended up, ironically, hurting the butterfly and preventing its natural growth to its mature form.

We see the importance of struggle and care to allow educational experiences to develop naturally both in the way Highlander Folk School developed (as an idea and as a place of

---

[34] Horton, *Haul*, 5-7
[35] Horton, "Building in the Democracy Mountains: The Legacy of the Highlander Center," 1986 interview with Danny Collum, reprinted in April 1986 issue of *Sojourners*, later printed in *The Myles Horton Reader*, 34-35

education in Tennessee) and in the way education was understood at Highlander. Beyond the history of Highlander, we need to better understand education as struggle and growth. As we see from these interviews with Myles Horton, education at Highlander is connected with a natural process of struggle that begins with attentiveness toward, and respect for, each person's unique experiences, situation and personality. You have to connect with people where they are.

A. Faith In People Where They Are
i. Finding the Seeds

Experience had taught Horton to have faith in the knowledge and skills of ordinary people, and in their ability to help each other when the setting is right. They didn't need to be lectured, as he explains: "The word *education* means drawing out. Education today means pouring in....Highlander's idea is still in the old sense of education, that there's already things in people you build on, you draw out. The idea of building on something. You build on what's in people to start with. And most of the theorizing and stuff to come out of Highlander has to do with empowering people by building on what's already there. The potential's in everyone. I've got two good eyes. I use both of my eyes. I use one to look at people where they are, at what is. And what's observable. That's the starting point. You've got to start at the bottom. You can't start up there. You've got to start at the foundation, not halfway up. You start with people's experience. That's one unique thing—the only unique thing—in the world, I guess, is individual experience. Our experience is unique to you, and mine is unique to me. So that's a sound basis on which to build, and it shows respect for the person."[36]

"Several years ago I was speaking at an alternative school conference. One of the people explained that Highlander was not a school in the sense of a college or any other kind of school because we didn't have classes, we didn't have credits, we didn't have this, that, and the other thing, and that we built on people's experiences instead of teaching them things they needed to know. And that's true. Highlander is not a school. But it is educational in the traditional meaning of the word 'educate,' which is to draw out instead of pour in. We think people become educated by analyzing their experience and learning from other people's experiences, rather than saying there's a certain body of knowledge that we need to give them."[37]

"If you were coming to a Highlander workshop I would look at you and I'd say where is this guy? I've got to get him to talk and find out where he is, find out something about his experience, what kind of person he is. I already know your background in general, because I grew up in the region, or a similar region, so I know some things about you already, but I don't know much. So my job is to try to size you up as a starting point, because I've got to start with you. You cannot move from where you ain't. You've got to move from where you are....That's the one eye that does that. Then you have to see the potential. There's a potential in everyone,

---

[36] Myles Horton, "A Different Kettle of Fish," 1989 unpublished interview with Susan Walker and Ike Coleman, printed in *The Myles Horton Reader,* 61

[37] Horton, "Building in the Democracy Mountains," in *The Myles Horton Reader*, 34

and my job is to have the imagination, as you talk and I get to know you, [of] seeing these little sprouts of interest, the seeds in there and understand a little bit more about you by using my imagination, from what I know about myself and about other people, so I can see some of your potential and start encouraging you to develop those potentials."[38]

It's important to understand that Horton is not merely describing a skill in finding someone's potential to fit a mold, but an attitude of respect for you as a human being: "And a lot of my encouragement depends on my genuine attitude toward you, my genuine respect for you as a human being and my faith that you have a potential to learn and to do things, my belief in you. And I have to demonstrate that not by telling you that [or] by making a speech about it but by the way I treat you. My attitude toward you has to be expressed in my actions. Because you can't learn anything about my attitude, you can only look and learn about my actions. My actions have got to be such that I say to you by my actions, I have confidence in you."[39]

ii. Cultivating the Seeds

Horton explained, however, that confidence was only a part of that second eye's work. Seeing potential didn't do much good if it didn't lead to cultivation, which is a difficult process and one that is unique to each individual. Because of that difficulty (and the importance of that growing process), care must be taken to show others that you, the instructor, have experienced educational growth before, and that you've felt the thrill and the pain of that experience, because that's what they will experience if they take this up. The instructor and student do not have the same experiences, nor do they necessarily have the same likes and dislikes, however: "if you see me get excited about the things I'm learning, my action then says to you, I want to share this enthusiasm for learning. In other words, your action has to be the thing that tells where you're coming from in terms of that second eye that looks toward the future. It's not too easy. Because half that three's underground, half of all plants are underground, half of anything practically is underground. And half of what people are is hidden inside, and you can't see it….And people have those microscopic roots too. Then they have sprouts, and seeds, and they have all levels, and that imagery helps me see what's inside people. And my job is to nourish them and water them and encourage them and give people hope and give them the fun of learning and the fun of developing. It's painful for people to grow. Growth is painful. It's painful for a seed to break out of the ground, and it's painful for a person to grow. And people have got to be introduced to the pain of growth, and not shy away from it, not be afraid of the pain, not be afraid to be unhappy, not be afraid to be stretched out, not be afraid to be laughed at, not be afraid to grow. Because that's part of growth. That's the way I kind of see education, that's my way of thinking about education. As kind of a natural, holistic way of looking at it. And the whole idea at Highlander is built around that theoretical concept, of the growth inside. And that means you can't try to shape people's lives, make them all alike. People grow at different speeds, have

---

[38] Horton, "A Different Kettle of Fish," in *The Myles Horton Reader*, 62
[39] *Ibid.*, 62

different interests, so you've got to take that into consideration, and you can't impose your ideas on people."[40]

After asserting that Highlander had been accused of feeding people propaganda, Horton explained that the school only brought out ideas that were already in the minds of the people who came to the workshops. School workers only helped people find their own ideas and perspectives and methods, their own "seeds" within themselves. By working together with teachers and students, each student's own seeds could be cultivated better.[41]

B. The Role of Conflict in Education

Horton also realized that when people speak in groups, there's bound to be disagreements and conflict, but this doesn't have to be negative: "If a situation arises, as it frequently does, that people in a group have diametrically opposed views, my interest is not in resolving that specific problem but in using the problem to involve the whole group in a discussion of the issues. Conflict sharpens the discussion. When years later we were holding workshops at Highlander about strip mining, one person might have said, 'Well, I don't see why we're horsing around here, the thing to do is get some dynamite and blow up the machinery,' while others would say, 'That's the wrong way to go at it, because we'd turn public opinion against us and we need the support of the people.' I know this dichotomy is something that everybody in the room had thought about. George Bernard Shaw once said that you only begin to solve a problem when you have two people who passionately believe in something state opposite views. That way you bring the thing out in the open." He explained further that it is best to allow the whole group to get involved in the conflict when it arose. The problem starts with two, but becomes the group's problem. It becomes obvious that it's more complicated than either of the two originally stated, and now that's out in the open for all to consider.[42]

C. Struggle and Growth for People Already Struggling

Horton, from the beginning, felt the need to help those at the bottom, not just because they were suffering the most, but because he did not believe real change could 'trickle down' from those more well-off: "All [Highlander projects] have been primarily for the workers, the unemployed, and minorities, who have been socialized to blame themselves for their plight, and to discount their experience as being of no worth. It is the experts and authorities that are supposed to have knowledge, not the common people. Consequently, they mistrust themselves and their fellow workers and defer to the self-proclaimed experts. Our students are painfully aware of their problems but not aware that, as a group, they can figure out most of the answers. They have been discouraged from making use of their experience and consider it of little educational value. Consequently, they have not deemed it worthwhile to analyze the one field of

---

40　*Ibid.*, 62-63
41　Horton, "The Adventures of a Radical Hillbilly: Part 1," in *The Myles Horton Reader*, 121
42　Horton, *Haul*, 47

learning where they are the true experts. They tend to look outside themselves, not only for answers, but also for motivation and empowerment, which can only come from within."[43]

Horton understood that people who are struggling, however ineffective that struggle may be, have a quality that is essential for succeeding: hope. As he explained, "It made no sense, however, to work with poor people who had given up hope. Only people with hope will struggle. The people who are hopeless are grist for the fascist mill. Because they have no hope, they have nothing to build on. If people are in trouble, if people are suffering and exploited and want to get out from under the heel of oppression, if they have hope that it can be done, if they can see a path that leads to a solution, a path that makes sense to them and is consistent with their beliefs and their experience, then they'll move. But it must be a path that they've started clearing. They've got to know the direction in which they are going and have a general idea of the kind of society they'd like to have. If they don't have hope, they don't even look for a path. They look for somebody else to do it for them.[44]

Horton explained that rather than push any particular program, Highlander tried to nurture that hope, to set it off and help it on its way, like someone trying to get a cake to rise. Hope, by itself, doesn't get things done, and feeling hopeful is only a fraction of the goal at Highlander. It is not a hope that someone else has the answers or will solve the problems, but a confident, energizing hope to work in mutual respect with others, with a faith that continues to guide you to success.[45]

D. Struggle and Nonviolence

Sparking and cultivating social change and collective action are, however, inherently dangerous activities. Horton and others at Highlander took part in union strike efforts, which were often violent or on the verge of violence. He explains that during the Wilder, Tennessee Strike, in 1933, he was determined to try to save the life of his friend, Barney Graham. Graham was the Wilder United Mine Workers president, and Horton not only knew which "gun thugs" were going to kill him, but he had pictures of them and information about their history. Trying to get people outside the Union to help protect Graham became an effort in futility which instigated a debate about violence and nonviolence: "Barney was one of those stubborn mountaineer union presidents and knew he was going to be killed, because that's what happened to people like him in those days. The union members knew he was going to be killed, too, and they were eager to do something about it....Then they asked me, 'Don't you think we ought to kill them?' I was presented with a real dilemma: should the gun thugs be killed, or should the gun thugs kill Barney. It wasn't any choice as I saw it. Since the union members asked me, I had to deal with that problem. I couldn't say, 'It's none of my business.' It was my business, because I was as concerned about the problem as they were. I said, 'Let's just talk it over and

---

[43] Myles Horton, "Influences on Highlander Research and Education Center, New Market, Tennessee, USA," 1983 presentation at the Grundtvig's Ideas in North America Conference at Holte, Denmark, printed in the conference proceedings and subsequently printed in *The Myles Horton Reader*, 26-27

[44] Horton, *Haul*, 44

[45] Horton, "Influences on Highlander Research and Education Center," in *The Myles Horton Reader*, 27

see what we're talking about. I don't mind seeing those gun thugs killed if that would be the end of it. They're going to kill a lot of people, but would that be the end of it? Do you kill two gun thugs and save Barney's life and there'd be no more to it, or would the killing of the gun thugs start a war and a lot of you'd be killed? To me that's the moral problem. When violence is used, somebody's going to be killed. The right thing to do is the lesser killing. How are we going to figure that out?"[46]

Horton maintains that he did not push the discussion one way or another, but just pointed out options and asked people to consider the consequences, and consider where their values took them. But he was sickened about any of the possibilities. When it was decided not to kill the gun thugs, Horton was drained, but still determined to, at the very least, make public the atrocity that was about to happen. He explains that, "I went home and collapsed. I was practically in a coma, but before I went to bed I wrote a story for one of the the [sic] labor presses at that time, in which I predicted the death of Barney Graham. I named the people who would shoot him and sent photographs of the thugs. I had their history and all the evidence. I added that I'd send a telegram later to give the final details and make any necessary changes. Then I sent a copy of the article and pictures to Alva Taylor, who at that time was a professor in the divinity school at Vanderbilt University. Barney was shot a week later, and all I had to do was give the date. There wasn't a word I had to change."[47]

Horton brought up this story about Barney Graham years later at a meeting of pacifists, asking them if it was better to allow one man to die, or kill two, given the specific men involved, but he couldn't get an answer. He explains, "They sat there for a long time and finally one of the ministers said, 'Well, I wouldn't get in a situation like that.' I asked the rest of them, 'Is that your position, that you'd stay away from the realities of life so you could be purists in your beliefs and not have to make decisions between violence and nonviolence?' I couldn't get anybody in the room to say anything other than that they wouldn't get themselves in such a situation. I said, 'That's just bald cowardice; somebody has to deal with problems like this. Certainly the miners in Wilder had to deal with it!"[48]

Horton also understood the temptation that some people had to advocate violence, especially if they didn't have to learn of the consequences first-hand. Regarding a talk at a college in California, where a local Communist group, with banners, criticized him, saying that he was betraying blacks by telling them to be nonviolent, Horton explained:
"According to this group, I was selling the people out, advising them wrongly. For them the only solution to the problem was armed action. They said blacks had to be armed, and they had to tell people they had to be armed, and they had to fight for it and so on. And I said, 'I appreciate that contribution to the discussion, and I'd like to make it clear that I think it's a

---

[46] Horton, *Haul*, 40
[47] *Ibid.*, 40-41
[48] *Ibid.*, 41

legitimate theory. It's an opinion of what's the right strategy, and I don't rule it out as something to discuss, I just happen to disagree with it. But,' I said, 'My position is, if you believe in something, then you act on it. Now, I say I believe in nonviolent protest, so I go on demonstrations. I'm willing to put myself on the line. I get beaten up, I get put in jail. I believe in racial equality and I want to demonstrate my belief by my actions. Since you're Marxists, you must believe in theory and practice, and I'm sure you agree with me that if you believe in something, you should act on it. When I get back to the South, I will arrange for you to be invited into Mississippi, where the struggle is now, and you can come down and demonstrate what it is you believe. You'll have a chance to present, in the most effective way, your argument. Give me your names so I can get in touch with you. Bring your guns and demonstrate to the black people the validity of your position.' I didn't get any responses, so I said, 'Could it be that you want black people to test out your ideas? And get killed, and find out whether it works or not? You wouldn't be doing that, would you?' They got up and walked out as a body. They didn't want to talk about it, but the answer was obvious: they wanted black people to test out their theories. I knew this answer all along. I just set it so I could educate people about practice and theory."[49]

E. Nonviolence in True Education

While Horton respected the realities that made violence and nonviolence matters of legitimate discussion and debate, his views about real education were consistent in asserting the primacy of nonviolence; not forcing ideas on other people. But nonviolence in education did not mean a free-for-all; there were rules at Highlander that were designed to respect everyone who had agreed, ahead of time, to discuss a specific problem or topic. That problem or topic was social in nature. Personal problems are important, of course, and they work their way into social problems at times, but transforming society requires a focus on social groups and social problems. So there were rules of one sort or another that the discussion leader found ways to enforce. As Horton describes, "In our workshops people can talk about anything that is appropriate to the problem they come with. The limits of discussion have nothing to do with freedom of speech, but with keeping to the topic we agreed on beforehand. Within that topic you can talk from any point of view. A person can say, 'As a Catholic I don't like this,' or 'As a Communist I don't like this,' or 'As a Klansman I don't like this,' but you can't come and make a partisan speech. All of the participants, equally, can discuss what everybody else is discussing. There can be no discrimination within the topic, and it is the role of the workshop leader to keep the group to its subject."[50]

Horton would have to turn away people who, claiming freedom of speech, wanted to rail about whatever was their pet topic. It didn't matter whether you were a fundamentalist minister or a communist. Horton describes a young man who'd been to Highlander before, returning as a member of a new, Communist organization that had just been recognized by Chairman Mao. He

---

[49] *Ibid.*, 142
[50] *Ibid.*, 154

wanted to tell a workshop group about this news. But after listening to him briefly, Horton let him know that the workshop was about what the people were interested in, not about what that one student wanted to lecture about. So, respect for everyone's freedom meant people disciplined themselves to keep to the topic at hand, allowing a wide diversity of approaches to that topic, never discriminating against discussion members, but always keeping it as the workshops center of gravity, as it were.[51]

Respect and a modicum of rules allowed the workshop to be substantive and focused on the practice of people learning from other people. But there were lots of items of cultural baggage that could become a barrier to such a workshop. Horton describes one incident that hinged on the word "negro," which was used more frequently before the term "black" began to be used for African-Americans. Horton explains: "At the workshop there was a tall white Texan. He was a nice guy and trying hard to fit in. He didn't have intellectual problems about antiracism, but he had cultural and social habits, and one of them was that he couldn't say the word "Negro" right. He didn't say 'nigger' because he knew that wasn't allowed in our workshops, so he'd say 'Neg-ro' or 'Ni-gro,' struggling to pronounce 'Negro.' The way he said it was riling up some of the people in the workshop and making it hard to get on with the issues we wanted to talk about. Charlie Hayes, who could be somewhat intimidating, finally said to him, 'Look, I've been trying to tell you to say 'Negro….You told me you grew up on a farm and you grew cotton.' The Texan asked Charlie why he brought that up, and Charlie said, 'Well, you can say 'grow,' can't you? Say 'grow!' So the Texan said 'grow' and Charlie said 'good,' and then he put his hand on the Texan's knee and asked him, 'What's this?' The Texan answered that it was his knee. Charlie continued: 'You don't have any trouble saying 'knee' and saying 'grow.' Now just say 'kneegrow.' That's Highlander's way of teaching. I hope that's enough, because my way is a little rougher.'"[52]

Furthermore, the learning at Highlander was not always "in the classroom" or even "in the discussion room." It happened more organically, as thoughts arouse in people's minds after a session, or as they talked casually over a meal or while having a swim. Horton felt that this less-direct kind of educational experience was so important that he wanted to make more room for it: "Still, we never had enough room for leisure time during workshop sessions. Once, Highlander got so packed with things, so overwhelmed by energy, by people trying to cover so much and crowd the schedule, that I announced my desire for somebody to take over my union problems class. I told the students I wanted to have a new job, I wanted to be professor of leisure. My job would be to see that there were periods of leisure that nobody could encroach on. I would have an hour of leisure a day, and also be the policeman to make sure that everyone had time to do anything that pleased them during that hour. Learning in society, outside school walls, takes place around the clock. It isn't restricted to specified times, certainly not to the same time of day for a limited number of minutes for, say, math, and then to another block of time for another subject. That's not life. Some of the best education at Highlander happened when the sessions

---

[51] *Ibid.*, 155
[52] *Ibid.*, 155-6

were over: at meals, on walks, and when people when back to their dormitories and sat around drinking coffee or whatever else they brought."⁵³

4) True Education Is Not Training For The Status Quo

Horton explains that education, as understood by contemporary academia is not what happens at Highlander Folk School, which is, instead, a place for genuine education. Education, at other places, amounts to indoctrination. Each type of political and economic society educates the young to become the cogs and wheels in their system, and keep it running that way. But the Highlander way was different and not focused on using people. "People are, you know, creative, you've got to allow them to do a lot of things that don't fit any kind of systems, and you've got to have a lot of deviations, to have a lot of pluralism. We believe in people keeping a lot of their old customs, and adding new ones. And we said, that's what enriches life....[T]he people have all this power, but it's suppressed by the public school system and the institutions. We, having loyalty [to] people and not the institutions, you know, always try to throw our weight on the side of the people..."⁵⁴

Horton and others at Highlander learned that teaching methods would also have to move away from the status quo. The status quo in pedagogy was an early barrier to working with the people who came to Highlander in the school's first year. "Although we accomplished some things by the end of that first year, we knew we really weren't reaching people the way we wanted to. The biggest stumbling block was that all of us at Highlander had academic backgrounds. We thought that the way we had learned and what we had learned could somehow be tailored to the needs of poor people, the working people of Appalachia....We ended up doing what most people do when they come to a place like Appalachia: we saw problems that we thought we had the answers to, rather than seeing the problems and the answers that the people had themselves. That was our basic mistake. Once you understood that, you don't have to have answers, and you can open up new ways of doing things....We thought all we'd have to do was go to them and say, 'What are your problems?' and they'd tell us....They thought it would be impolite to ask us to do something that we couldn't, and that it would hurt our feelings. Sometimes they didn't say anything at all."⁵⁵

Horton explained their early difficulties as part of the then accepted pedagogy of putting theory before practice, both in importance and in chronology: "When we first started Highlander, we had ideas that we tried to apply to a situation. We started by moving from theory to practice. It took us only a few months to learn that we were starting the wrong way, because we weren't reaching the people. We realized it was necessary to learn how to learn from these people, so we started with the practical, with the things that were, and we moved from there to test our theories and our ways of thinking. We reversed the usual process; instead of coming from the top down and going from the theoretical to the practical, trying to force the theory on the practical, we learned you had to take what people perceive their problems to be, not what we perceive their

---

53   *Ibid.*, 160
54   Horton, "The Adventures of a Radical Hillbilly, Part 1," in *The Myles Horton Reader,* 120-121
55   Horton, *Haul,* 68

problems to be. We had to learn how to find out about the people, and then take that and put it into a program. Sometimes that knowledge ties into some theories, but if the theories don't fit the practice, then you say the theory is wrong, not the other way around. Before, we had been saying that if the practice didn't fit the theory, the people were wrong, and we tried to force the people into the theory."[56]

5) How True Education is Cultivated at Highlander

The focus of education at Highlander is on the social environment of the people who call for the workshop. There is a real effort to cultivate cordiality, to have activities together, not a lot of pre-planned structure, but structure that allows people to feel comfortable, respected, respectful and genuine. Horton often describes it as a circle of learners: "I think of an educational workshop as a circle of learners. 'Circle' is not an accidental term, for there is no head of the table at Highlander workshops; everybody sits around in a circle. The job of the staff members is to create a relaxed atmosphere in which the participants feel free to share their experiences. Then they are encouraged to analyze, learn from and build on these experiences. Like other participants in the workshops, staff members are expected to share experiences that relate to the discussions, and sources of information and alternative suggestions. they have to provide more information than they will be able to work into the thinking process of the group, and often they must discard prepared suggestions that become inappropriate to the turn a workshop has taken. Consultants who were brought to Highlander at considerable expense were sometimes not allowed to make presentations, because what they had to offer did not provide answers to the problems raised by the participants. Often we had to send back movies and pamphlets without using them. Each session had to take its own form and develop according to the students' needs."[57]

A. A Fluid Method or No Method At All

At first glance, it is difficult to see a method in the way things work at Highlander, as Horton explains, "Highlander does not have a neat, predictable pattern of activities. We have not moved in a straight line toward our goal. We have been more like the Tennessee River, which starts nearby on its journey to the ocean. We zig and zag to get around obstacles to take advantage of an easier route, and like the winding river, we are not self-sufficient, but constantly being reinforced, refreshed, and nurtured by students, new teachers, and coworkers."[58] While he understood the importance of people working together in organizations, that it gave them a power they did not have as individuals, but he was concerned that organizations can become sterile and rigid after a while, no longer serving people, but using them in an unhelpful manner.[59]

B. "First Enliven, then Enlighten": The Importance of Music at Highlander

---

[56] *Ibid.*, 140
[57] *Ibid.*, 150
[58] Horton, "Influences on Highlander Research and Education Center," in *The Myles Horton Reader*, 27-28
[59] Horton, *Haul*, 49

The emphasis on music at Highlander was not merely as a recreational pastime, but as part of the vitality of the educational experience itself. Music, drama and other arts had been part of the Danish folk schools that Horton had studied and visited as the idea of Highlander took root, and with the help of his wife, Zilphia Maen."[60], and others, Horton made sure there was singing, dancing and drama at Highlander. They followed the lead of Kristen Kold (of the Danish Folk Schools), and the maxim 'First enliven, then enlighten.' You need to raise someone's spirits, their confidence, their pride and connection to others before education can take root. Otherwise, you treat them disrespectfully, trying to force them to learn and participate when they don't feel the need to do so: "At Highlander music enlivened. Classes on specific union problems enlightened. Singing together and giving plays had equal importance at Highlander residential workshops with courses on contract negotiation, parliamentary law, public speaking, or union problems. Nearly one hundred labor plays were written by Highlander staff members or students between 1935 and 1952, and countless songs about working-class struggles were compiled."[61]

As with most things at Highlander, it was not a specific methodology or program that carried the day, it was about the people: "[Zilphia] had studied music at the College of the Ozarks and possessed a special quality of warmth which enabled her to relate to differing people. She could help people forget their personal problems and, at the same time, help them understand the problems of others. People who wouldn't usually sing with strangers would sing with her. There was a quality about her that inspired trust."[62]

She and Pete Seeger (folk singer and activist who visited Highlander from time to time) took a song by two South Carolina union members (names now unknown), and with a little tweaking, gave the labor movement, and later the civil rights movement, "We Shall Overcome."

In one interview, she expressed her feelings and thoughts about music: "'Music is the language of and to life. Music has been too generally thought of as an art form for leisure time, performed and enjoyed by and for the chosen few. The people can be made aware that many of the songs about their everyday lives—songs about their work, hopes, their joys and sorrows—are songs of merit. This gives them a new sense of dignity and pride in their cultural heritage. Their lives can be enriched also by learning folk songs of other nationalities. The folk song grows out of reality. It is this stark reality and genuineness which gives the folk song vitality and strength….'"[63]

C. Holistic and Service-oriented Approach of Highlander

As is evident from the historical background of Highlander, Horton was inspired by his life with family and neighbors in the Tennessee mountains: "If you grew up poor like I did in the mountains and the rural South, you tend to think of the totality of things that make up life.

---

[60] Adams, *Seeds*, 73
[61] *Ibid.*, 72
[62] *Ibid.*, 73
[63] *Ibid.*, 76

Everybody struggled to make a living. Most people in my culture went to church; there wasn't much else to do. When I was growing up there were only two places that kids could meet people, school or church. Activities had to do with either of these. If you weren't in school or church, then you didn't have any social life. So it wasn't a matter of making some decision about this….So I grew up thinking of those things being integral—all part of life. The singing, the square dancing, and the fights—all were part of life. It wasn't as segmented as in more civilized or advanced society. So I always thought more holistically….I never thought of culture as being limited to the fine arts although they are part of culture."[64]

Horton saw culture as the enriching aspects of life, whatever they were, and decided that they had to be part of the Highlander experience: "Music was a part of everything. Music was always a very important part of things. In my life pictures, not art but pictures such as calendars or any kinds of picture, were important. They enriched life. A picture was something important. I'm not saying that I like now the things that I liked then; I don't. But then it had a meaning. I like poetry for reasons that I don't know. Poetry was always important to me. I don't want to leave any of those things out. That's why I want to include them at Highlander. *Without culture in its broader sense, you have a tendency to make intellectualization a bloodless kind of exercise.* It becomes a kind of a gymnastic exercise. It has very little to do with life. You have to keep it tied in with the cultural side to have meaning. *The intellectual part should serve the cultural; not the cultural serve the intellectual.* The culture is a totality."[65]

This helps argue against the charge that Highlander was a place for pushing union or civil rights propaganda. The cultural lives of people were served by theories, methods, and programs devised for that service. People were not bent to serve ideas and methods, ideas and methods were bent to serve people. In fact, that explains some of the difficulty that others have had in try to duplicate the Highlander experience.

Because it is focused on serving people in the fullness of their cultural lives, its workshops have to be tailored to unique people, places and problems. Propaganda is any effort to duplicate something (usually an idea, a method, a goal) which can be expressed abstractly and duplicated endlessly, but people's individual lives are concrete and unique, and an educational effort directed toward helping them help each other must change and shift from person to person and community to community. Taken in their cultural lives, each person and each community are unique, valuable and worthy of respect. Hence, the approach must reflect that. In a discussion about the educational ideas of Paulo Freire (an educator and activist with whom Horton shared some similarities), Horton noted that Freire's ideas and methods were unlike his own in the sense that they could be used as techniques abstracted from unique people and situations. In other words, they could be used for, or against, the interests of common people.[66]

64　　Horton, "Ideas That Have Withstood the Test of Time," in *The Myles Horton Reader*, 51
65　　*Ibid.*, 51-52 (my emphasis)
66　　*Ibid.*, 55

D. Trust, Compassion, Respect, and Awareness as a Methodology

Horton explained the genesis of a method with no fixed, duplicable method as practicing what you preach; not just preaching. Furthermore, you trust that people can change; you have faith they can change, and after a while, you've seen it. As he explains: "How people learn is a miracle. I don't understand how it takes place....I have known Klansman who come to Highlander. They say, 'I will eat with these niggers, but I want you to know that I am a Klansman.' I have had them leave changed, and they are still changed today....To make it happen is easier than to understand it. Human beings are so darn sensitive and complicated. There is still that great mystery there."[67] The best method is whatever worked best for particular people in particular situations. As he explained, "This is better than a method that you clamp onto every situation and force people into it like you are torturing them."[68]

When asked about what social and cultural issues are going to be significant in helping particular people learn, Horton tells the story of the literacy programs in the Citizenship school in the Sea Islands off the South Carolina coast: "I talk to the people and get a feel of it—their unspoken sense of it. Before we started the Citizenship School program, I went down to the Sea Islands and stayed with Esau. It was all a blur. Yet I was determined to find a way to help Esau because it was a real problem. If you are going to have a democracy, people have a right to vote. If they are required to read and write to vote, then you are going to have to teach them to read and write so they can vote. That is aside from being interested in education for education's sake. It is kind of a moral imperative to me. But I couldn't figure it out. I stayed off and on for a couple of months and talked to the people out in the rice fields, watched them fish, when out and helped them with the work, got out to visit, and went to their churches. Gradually, I got to understand them. They got used to me because I was a friend of Esau. I finally got the sense of people. Then I saw why it is that they didn't want to read and write."[69]

At first, Horton thought it was lack of motivation because there were no economic or political opportunities that reading and writing would serve, but when Esau ran for office, there was a reason to get registered to vote, yet, it didn't work. They had teachers down there but no one wanted to learn: "I started to try to analyze the situation and came up with this whole bit of dignity. They didn't treat them with respect; they didn't treat them with dignity. They treated them like little kids. They were contemptuous of them. They actually put them in seats for children; they called them daddy longlegs, these big old lanky people sitting in a chair for first graders. They just treated them like dirt. So that became obvious that you have to treat people with respect."[70]

So Horton, like a cultural anthropologist doing participant observation, took part in daily activities and got to know people in the Sea Islands, as someone taking part in their daily,

---

[67] *Ibid.*, 56
[68] *Ibid.*, 53-54
[69] *Ibid.*, 56
[70] *Ibid.*, 57

cultural lives: "What I am trying to say is that I don't sit down and try to figure the thing out in my head. I try to get in and get a sense of it. Now I use the same kind of sensing and feeling about the other problems....I used to go out on the farm where the people worked, and where there was the 'man.' I saw that they couldn't watch the scales; they couldn't figure anything, they knew they were being gypped. I was beginning to see some of the conflict situations and see some of the points where you could stir them up, get them angry, and get them to see the injustices. You have to find points of injustice that people will recognize as injustice."[71]

E. Learning Circles: the Lack of Hierarchy

In addition to efforts to "get to know" people in their cultural situation (when invited, Horton did not push his way into working with folks), respect for people was also facilitated by the physical layout of discussion rooms as well as the physical, living-together of the workshop experience at Highlander, as Horton explained: "What we have always done, I got from the Indians. They always sit around in circles so that there is nothing hierarchical. They did have a chief, but he was on the same level. What I always tried to do was to break the hierarchical situation so that everyone was a part of the learning circle. If we are part of the same circle, we are all learning. Our experiences may be different, but we all are learning. It was just a way of having everyone equal, and so they could see each other. The comfort is in the rocking chairs we use. Physical is important: sleeping together, having people together, having people eat together, and having people talk together. Togetherness is important. The residentialness of it is important. You couldn't go to a hotel and have a Highlander workshop....You couldn't go to a place where you have a big building with several other groups meeting and where you meet in one corner. It has to be contained, unified, concentrated to get the sense of the people who are there. We get them physically away from their everyday life so they can begin to think about something that is terribly important."[72] Sitting in a circle established that the meeting was not formed around a hierarchy. Teachers were facilitators who kept discussion on track without introducing ideas that came from outside the group; but they were also participants in the discussion as well, learning as much as anyone else.[73]

So Horton's 'method' had at least several phases, when it worked well. It began with relationships which led others to ask for the help of folks at Highlander. Then a respectful period of getting-to-know the people who were asking for help; participating in their lives, listening to them without preconceptions, treating them with dignity. Finally, there was the actual workshop at Highlander Folk School, at which people were treated to an environment in which concentrated, respectful discussion could take place with the intent on helping them learn from one another and discover ways they could help one another.

---

[71] *Ibid.*, 57
[72] *Ibid.*, 50
[73] Horton, "Influences on Highlander Research and Education Center," in *The Myles Horton Reader*, 27

Those people who are used to having hierarchy in meetings and organizations often become comfortable with the idea that the opinions of those at the top are more important that of those at the bottom. A lack of hierarchy, to such people, may suggest a lack of any important ideas at all, since none of them 'stand above' the others, as they do in a hierarchy. But at Highlander, they found that the lack of hierarchy could, actually, result in an appreciation of the importance of each person's views. It starts with the mutual respect that a lack of hierarchy can help make possible, and the willingness to respect the subjects that someone doesn't want to discuss, as well as the willingness to try to discover how they perceive themselves and their own problems. Horton explains: "It's very important that you understand the difference between your perception of what people's problems are and their perception of them. You shouldn't be trying to discover your perception of their perception. You must find a way to determine what their perception is. You can't do it by psychoanalyzing or being smart. You have to ask yourself what you know about their experience and cultural background that would help in understanding what they're saying. You need to know more about them than they know about themselves. This sounds like a paradox, but the reason they don't know themselves fully is that they haven't learned to analyze their experience and learn from it. When you help them to respect and learn from their own experience, they can know more about themselves than you do. I learned another important lesson that first year at Monteagle [site of Highlander in Tennessee]. We bought a hundred-pound sack of beans and a bushel of whole wheat that we'd grind up and that's about all we'd eat. People were poor—we were all poor. One day I found a sack of potatoes on the front porch. I knew where those potatoes came from because there were only one or two people in the community who grew them, and I also knew they were very poor and had young children. My first reaction was 'I can't keep these potatoes, I'll just take them back and tell them how much I appreciate it.' But I got to thinking, 'What a goddamned elitist person! You give your clothes to people, and you enjoy doing it, yet you would deny them the privilege of giving something to you.'"[74]

That 'putting yourself on the same level with others' attitude meant learning to read the nonverbal cues that people would make as you spoke, respecting someone's silence and living with them, the way they live, so you could begin to feel what it is like for them to live in that situation. Horton explains: "The significance of all this was that it prepared me to be in the circle of learners and to respect other people's ideas. As well as giving my ideas, I was receiving ideas, and this helped convince people that I sincerely respected all they had to contribute. People have to believe that you genuinely respect their ideas and that your involvement with them is not just an academic exercise. If I hadn't had these rather emotional, traumatic experiences of learning, to the point where it became a part of me, I couldn't have been natural about saying, 'Look, you don't really appreciate how much you learn from your experience, and how valuable that is, because you've never been encouraged to believe it's important.'"[75]

---

[74] Horton, *Haul*, 70-71
[75] *Ibid.*, 71

The lack of hierarchy allows people to help each other realize their problems with greater clarity and, collaboratively, work toward solutions. As Horton explains, "There were no given answers to the problems we dealt with, and we don't pretend to have any. They have to be worked out in the process of struggling with the problem. The knowledge needed for the solution has to be created....Highlander gives them a *chance* to explore what they know and what some people we bring in as a resources can share with them. Then they have to go back home and test what they learn in action."[76]

Sometimes, people do not see the larger context of their problems and think they are only personal problems that they, for some reason, cannot solve. By meeting, talking, and living together, they begin to see how these are social problems that require a more collective response. Horton explains, "They must know that they have problems which can't be solved on a personal level, that their problems are social, collective ones which take an organized group to work on. For this reason, an individual can't come to a Highlander workshop with a personal problem. People have to be selected by their organizations and report back to the organizations that sent them. For example, Rosa Parks came to a Highlander workshop shortly before she refused to move so that a white man could have her seat on a bus. She was sent to the workshop by E.D. Nixon, Alabama NAACP president and vice president of the Brotherhood of Sleeping Car Porters, and by Virginia Durr, a white woman from Montgomery, Alabama, who had been fighting racial segregation for years….At the end of our workshops we reviewed and critiqued the sessions and then asked the participants what they were going to do when they got home. Rosa Parks said that she didn't know what she could do in 'the cradle of the Confederacy,' but at a later workshop she described her first workshop experience: 'At Highlander, I found out for the first time in my adult life that this could be a unified society, that there was such a thing as people of different races and backgrounds meeting together in workshops, and living together in peace and harmony. It was a place I was very reluctant to leave. I gained there the strength to persevere in my work for freedom, not just for blacks, but for all oppressed people.'"[77]

F. Grassroots Leadership: the Lack of Charismatic Leaders

The goal of this workshop style was true education and grassroots leadership, but not charismatic leadership, as Horton explains: "The only problem I have with movements has to do with my reservations about charismatic leaders. There's something about having one that can keep democracy from working effectively. But we don't have movements without them. That's why I had no intellectual problem supporting King as a charismatic leader."[78]

Horton describes how he, himself, felt the temptation to become a charismatic leader during a strike in Lumberton, North Carolina in 1937. The strikers were from a mix of racial backgrounds: African-American, European-American, even Native-American, and the strike

---

[76] *Ibid.*, 148
[77] *Ibid.*, 148-150
[78] *Ibid.*, 120

went on for months. To keep up their enthusiasm, Horton helped organize music and singing; but finally he started giving speeches; there was nothing else to do. He even started to like it; being able to hold the attention of an audience who appreciated what he was saying. But the power he felt himself wielding began to worry him. As he explained: "One night I got to thinking about this, and said to myself, 'This is scary. This is the kind of thing I don't believe in, this is dangerous. Even if it's doing some good for the people, it certainly isn't doing me any good, and it's a temptation.' That's when I thought about the Lord's Prayer, which doesn't say, 'Save me from doing evil,' it says, 'Lead me not into temptation,' It's the temptation you've got to watch, and there I was being tempted by the power that comes from charisma. My speaking certainly wasn't developing local leaders."[79]

Horton explained that he saw this danger in Martin Luther King Jr.'s leadership of the SCLC, and even told him about it. He felt that Dr. King was much more than a charismatic leader, and did more things than just make speeches and point fingers; but he was so good in his leadership that Horton didn't see others finding their own voice of leadership; their own style and authority: "Sometimes they got discouraged, because the tree was too big and too dense for undergrowth. One of the criticisms I made to him was 'You are so much the powerful leader that it's hard for people who work for you to have a role they can grow in. You could spend time making room under the tree and developing other leaders to take on some of the responsibilities.' Martin would say, 'In my mind I know that has to be done, and it is happening,' but from my perspective, it looked as if he had never developed anybody who could take his place after he was killed. Although there were a lot of people whose leadership was developed, they weren't widely known....The best his replacements could do was try to create carbon copies of him, not become leaders in their own right. When it came to original thinking and being creative, people would say, 'Well, what would Martin have done?' and try to do the same thing. To me, this was a great weakness in the movement. My point is that he never did get around to really doing what he knew was needed. I think that's a very difficult thing for a charismatic leader to do."[80]

Highlander's Goal: Real Democracy and Social Change

There is thought and care in everything at Highlander, and in the Highlander idea, from the physical layout of discussion rooms, to common meals and meal preparation, to the singing and dancing, and the effort to ask questions that help people bring out their concerns, problems, hope and solutions. The goal is what Horton called Real Democracy: "My goal is democracy, not capitalism, or socialism, or communism or something else, but democracy. A real democracy, where people control their lives....It's not up to me to try to mastermind that. I think it's up to all of us to share our hopes and our dreams and our ideas as far as we can. But it's not something you try to impose on people."[81]

---

[79] *Ibid.*, 120-2
[80] *Ibid.*, 126-7
[81] Horton, "A Different Kettle of Fish," in *The Myles Horton Reader*, 63

The emphasis on democracy does not eliminate the role of the educator, but it does change it. The educator needs to be part of an effort to set the most helpful environment for discussion, deliberation and consensus, without aiming for a particular outcome or trying to rush the group's process. As Horton explains, "The best teachers of poor and working people are the people themselves. They are the experts on their own experiences and problems. The students who came to Highlander brought their own ways of thinking and doing. We tried to stimulate their thinking and expose them to consultants, books and ideas, but it was more important for them to learn how to learn from each other. Then they could go back to their communities and keep on learning from each other and from their actions. Since our workshops were brief—a couple of weeks or even a long weekend—they had to be tied to learning that had already taken place and was related to a problem they were still working on. We served as a catalytic agent to hasten the learning process. It goes without saying that in our concept of education, there were no grades and no examinations. We also claimed no neutrality in presenting facts and ideas. What we sought was to set people's thinking apparatus in motion, while at the same time trying to teach and practice brotherhood and democracy."[82]

Horton describes it as a challenging process of struggle and growth; in particular, trusting that the people you try to help will grow: "Now at Highlander we had enough experience to know that people do have that capacity. In the early CIO days we saw people who had never heard of unions become good union members, take on fights, and develop and grow as people. In the civil rights movement we saw people come out of the fields and get in the voter registration line and be beaten up and shot at and become leaders and run for office and get elected. Since we've seen that, we don't think of ourselves as utopian. My job is to try to provide opportunities for people to grow (not to make them grow, because no one can do that), to provide a climate which nurtures islands of decency, where people can learn in such a way that they continue to grow. I grew up on a farm, so I know about growing things. And I still work in my garden. Gardening helps remind me how growing happens. Your job as a gardener or as an educator is to know that the potential is there and that it will unfold. Your job is to plant good seeds and nurture them until they get big enough to grow up, and not to smother them while they are growing. You shouldn't overwater them, overfertilize them or overwork them. And when bugs get on the plants, you've got to get rid of them so the plants can continue to grow. People have a potential for growth; it's inside, it's in the seeds. This kind of potential cannot guarantee a particular outcome, but it's what you build on. What people need are experiences in democracy, in making democratic decisions that affect their lives and communities."[83]

We should not forget about the difficulty that accompanies real growth, and real democracy by extension. These difficulties are not those of being forced to do something from the outside, but the difficulties of responding to your personal judgments regarding your experiences, as well as weighing and reconsidering those judgments in light of the judgments of others. They are also the difficulties that can lead to changes in the structure of society itself.

---

[82] Horton, *Haul*, 152
[83] *Ibid.*, 132-3

They are big goals and big difficulties, but those are the kind you want to take on. As Horton explains: "There is a popular theory that if you give people simple enough goals that they can reach without too much effort, they will get a sense of success, and that success will build them up. I think that's a lot of malarkey. If a goal isn't something very difficult, all that people will learn to do is to tackle little problems. You can't develop valuable leadership if you don't teach people that they can deal with big problems. At Highlander we wanted people to deal with how to change society, not with smaller issues such as trying to get a street light or a road crossing sign installed. Those issues are important, but they are not ways to transform society. We only invited people who we perceived were dealing with basic changes in the structure of society."[84]

There are many examples of Highlander cultivating grassroots leadership and collective responses to social problems, but one good example Horton describes is the work of black and white women in West Virginia, who were welfare recipients from a rural, coal mining part of the state. They had been told to just follow orders from a national organization, but they needed solutions to more local problems in their state. After four days at Highlander, they decided they needed to hold workshops in West Virginia for organizing their own state organization. So Horton and others gave them the wisdom of their experience with workshops.[85] These women went on to build an organization of almost a thousand people, and were able to get help from specialists, when necessary. Furthermore, they generated cohesiveness and stuck together. Three years later, when the West Virginia legislature set up a committee to consider new codes and programs, the women, who by then were better informed about these matters than any committee member, insisted on being heard, but were initially denied. So they let the committee know that if they could not take part, they would close down the legislature. As Horton explains, "The next day miners started pouring in by the hundreds, and in no time the legislative committee invited the women to testify. They had their bill and a strategy, and the new law passed by the legislature included many ideas the welfare organization had formulated in its workshop. This illustrates the role of education in extending democracy."[86]

---

[84] *Ibid.*, 146-7
[85] *Ibid.*, 166-7
[86] *Ibid.*, 168

Appendix IV:
Primary Readings
for The Struggle for Civil Rights

While *A Testament of Hope* is the primary book for the ideas and methods which are debated in *The Struggle for Civil Rights*, other readings from other figures in the Civil Rights Movement are equally important. The primary readings should not be understood to exhaust the field of helpful accounts of how ideas and methods were put into practice and modified and debated, but rather should be understood as a solid foundation from which further studies may be made. Participants were keen to consider how they made their message heard. The methods of raising awareness and cultivating change were often debated as much as the ideas and policies which those methods were meant to promote, in order to find new ways to combat old problems.

Reading Selections from *A Testament of Hope: The Essential Writings and Speeches of Martin Luther King Jr.*, ed. by James M. Washington (New York: HarperCollins Publishers, 1986, 1991)
Selections for *Dorchester 1963: The Struggle for Nonviolent Tension*
Ch. 1 "Nonviolence and Racial Justice" (1957) pp5-9
Ch. 3 "The Power of Nonviolence" (1958) pp12-15
Ch. 4 "An Experiment in Love (1958) pp16-20
Ch. 7 "The Social Organization of Nonviolence (1959) pp31-34
Ch. 8 "Pilgrimage to Nonviolence" (1960) pp35-40
Ch. 9 "Suffering and Faith" (1960) pp41-42
Ch. 10 "Love, Law, and Civil Disobedience" (1961) pp43-53
Ch. 20 "The Case Against 'Tokenism'" (1962) pp106-111
Ch. 22 "The Ethical Demands of Integration" (1963) pp117-125
Ch. 36 "I Have a Dream" (1963) pp217-220

Selections for *Memphis 1966: The Struggle for Black Power*
Ch. 11 "Nonviolence: the Only road to Freedom" (1966) pp54-61
Ch. 32 "Next Stop: The North" (1965) pp189-194
Ch. 43 "The Drum Major Instinct" (1968) pp259-267
Ch. 46 "Letter from Birmingham City Jail" (1963) pp289-302
Ch. 54 "A Tough Mind and a Tender Heart: Ch. 1 from *The Strength to Love*" (1963) pp491-497
Ch. 54 "Our God Is Able: from Ch. 13 from *The Strength to Love*" (1963) pp507-509
Ch. 54 "Antidotes For Fear: Ch. 14 from *The Strength to Love*" (1963) pp509-517
Ch. 56 "Black Power: Ch. 2 from *Where Do We Go from Here: Chaos or Community*" (1967) pp569-597
Ch. 57 "Conscience and the Vietnam War: from Ch. 2 from *The Trumpet of Conscience*" (1967) pp634-640

Primary Readings for *The Struggle for Civil Rights*
(not in *A Testament of Hope*)

Readings for both *Dorchester 1963* and *Memphis 1966*:

I. Texts of the 13th, 14th and 15th Amendments to the Constitution of the United States of America

II. from *In Search of Democracy: The NAACP Writings of James Weldon Johnson, Walter White, and Roy Wilkins (1920-1977)*, ed. by Sondra Kathryn Wilson (Oxford: Oxford University Press, 1999)

James Weldon Johnson
    "The N.A.A.C.P.'s Fight Against Lynching" pp102-105
    "Achievements and Aims of the N.A.A.C.P." pp114-116
    "The Militant N.A.A.C.P." pp116-121

Roy Wilkins
    "The War against the United States" pp365-370
    "The Meaning of the Sit-Ins" pp399-406
    "Sail our N.A.A.C.P. Ship 'Steady as She Goes'" pp422-429
    "Toward a Single Society" pp430-436

Readings for *Dorchester 1963*:

III. from *The Eyes on The Prize Civil Rights Reader*, ed. by Glayborne Carson, David J. Garrow, Gerald Gill, Vincent Harding and Darlene Clark Hine (New York: Penguin Books, 1991)

Robert F. Williams
    "Is Violence Necessary to Combat Injustice? For the Positive: Williams Says 'We Must Fight Back'" pp110-112

Franklin McCain
    "Interview with Franklin McCain" pp114-116

Rev. James Lawson
    "Student Nonviolent Coordinating Committee Statement of Purpose" pp119-120
    "Eve of Nonviolent Revolution?" pp130-132"

Readings for *Dorchester 1963* (continued):

Ella J. Baker
    "Bigger than a Hamburger" pp120-122

Robert Zellner
    "Interview with Robert Zellner" pp127-130

Charles Sherrod
    "Organizing in Albany, Georgia" pp138-139

Bernice Johnson Reagon
    "Interview with Bernice Reagon" pp143-145

Readings for *Memphis 1966*:

James Forman
    "SNCC-SCLC Relations" pp217-220

Malcolm X
    "Message to the Grass Roots" pp248-261

Stokely Carmichael
    "What We Want" pp282-286

IV.   from *The Rhetoric of Black Power*, ed. by Robert L. Scott and Wayne Brockriede (New York: Harper & Row, Publishers, 1969)

Stokely Carmichael
    "Stokely Carmichael Explains Black Power to a Black Audience in Detroit" pp84-95
    "Stokely Carmichael Explains Black Power to a White Audience in Whitewater, Wisconsin" pp96-111